Journeying Together

A joint autobiography

John & Anne Twisleton

Copyright © 2023 John & Anne Twisleton
All rights reserved.
ISBN: 979-8860972223

Contents

Title page		
Copyright		1
Introduction		4
1	A passion for Chemistry	6
2	Artist in the making	12
3	A priestly calling	18
	Photo album	24
4	Missionaries	34
5	Marriage in Guyana	40
6	Sent to Coventry	46
7	London calling	52
	Anne's paintings	58
8	Sussex-by-the-sea	116
9	Active retirement	122
	Photo album	128
10	Journeying with Alzheimer's	138
Conclusion		144
Appendix 1 - Family trees		146
Appendix 2 - Books, blogs and radio work		156
Appendix 3 - Timeline		169

Introduction

Thirty five years of marriage is worth writing about. That is not always the case, sadly, but in our case we have had a good journey so far despite the ups and downs. John is more of a book writer than Anne who, like her late mother Doris, is a copious letter writer. Shaping up our story is more due to him than her and is determined by six places we have lived since our marriage solemnised in 1988 by an Amerindian priest in Guyana, South America. Prefaced by our individual stories the plot moves from Guyana to Coventry, London and Sussex building momentum as our sons enter the picture with their families: Dave and Denise with Tori and Robyn, John Junior and James and Rebecca set to be married next year.

'Journeying Together' has significance beyond being a double autobiography serving family and friends. Here is the trajectory of a Yorkshire Dalesman heading south to become a Sussex Downsman. The book invites readers to enter with us the beauty and challenge of Guyana's interior helped by Anne's paintings for which its pages make good occasion for a display. It celebrates with John another marriage, that of science and Christianity, as well as his exercise of the priesthood in Guyana and the post-Christian culture of the UK. In Anne's story we present the benefits of social engagement tackling illiteracy with Volunteer Reading Help and poverty with our local Family Support Work.

Our book concludes naturally with where we are now in Haywards Heath, West Sussex touching on our current situation living with dementia. This is a growing challenge across cultures, for us specifically that of living with Alzheimer's disease. We will touch on Anne's recent experience and John's as her carer supported by John Junior, family and friends. Whether you pick up this book as family, friend or without personal knowledge of us we hope you find diversion, food for thought and something to warm the heart in the following pages.

John & Anne Twisleton　　　　　　　　**October 2023**

1 A passion for Chemistry

I was born in Doncaster in 1948 and named John Fiennes. I was the first child of Greg Twisleton, Midland Bank manager at Thorne and Elsie (née Vickers), who'd previously been Domestic Science teacher at Thorne Grammar School. Greg and Elsie were from the other end of Yorkshire, Settle and neighbouring Hellifield and had moved east for work near Doncaster. Greg's parents Greg and Jane had run a shop in Settle Marketplace. Over 20 years older than Elsie, Greg had been asked to 'keep an eye' on Elsie who visited him and his widowed mother Jane at their bungalow, 41 Southfield Road, Thorne. From those visits romance blossomed so that on Mrs Twisleton's death another Mrs Twisleton appeared with Elsie marrying Greg at her home Church of St Aidan, Hellifield on 3rd February 1948

After preaching at Belsize Park in the 1990s I recall a former bank clerk at Thorne approaching me to tell me how well he remembered my birth all those years back. Greg's pride at his first son's birth on 29 November 1948 clearly impacted his staff at Midland Bank who were very attached to him. Greg served at Thorne until his retirement in 1963. My memories of childhood include that of going to St Nicholas Church and then down the hill to check the bank with daddy accompanied by my younger brother Tony. We boys once set off the bank alarm bringing a visit from the police!

Among my earliest memories was watching the Coronation of Queen Elizabeth II in 1953 on our new television with most of Southfield Road, as well as seeing the enormous Council estate built up at the end of the road. Elsie and Greg had gifts of hospitality and friendship which became implanted in their sons who attended the Green Top Primary School where I had a best friend, Christopher Pavlosky. Our family were privileged to have a car and a caravan, first at Skipsea and then at Bridlington, venues of many happy holidays often in the company of the Oglesby family. Life changed for me at just short of 11 when I was sent to Catteral Hall at Giggleswick School to board followed two years later by my brother Tony. This decision expressed dad's determination that his sons would get the best academic start in life. Greg was himself an Old Giggleswickian.

At Giggleswick I made special friends with Robert Blewitt, Edward Harland, Tony Haygarth, Roger Miller, Martin Moore and John Ormerod. I remember 'Harland' telling me the facts of life whilst sitting in the rockery at Catteral Hall! This was revisited officially during Confirmation Classes when housemaster John Dean expanded his explanation of the Virgin Birth. Afterwards, to our great embarrassment, Dean kept back Blewitt and I, as in his judgement maybe more sensible boys, to check with us he'd put the facts of life straight! Among my teachers was the florid Russell Harty and Richard Whitely, near contemporary, was in Shute House with me, both men later becoming television personalities. Like Russell, my mother Elsie was a friend of playwright Alan Bennett. In later years I came to enjoy many return visits to preach in Giggleswick's beautiful chapel, especially on the 500th anniversary of the school in 2012, and year by year since then.

I won a scholarship in Chemistry to St John's College, Oxford in 1966. This achievement built both from the inspiration of my teacher Bill Brocklebank and my own home Chemical experimentation with friend Roger Miller. This occasionally filled 1 Stackhouse Lane, Giggleswick with brown clouds of nitrogen dioxide! By then my father had retired and moved back to his and Elsie's native Yorkshire Dales making Tony and I day boys at Gigg school instead of boarders. Tony was more gregarious and sporty at Gigg. I was a quiet, studious boy who liked walking, encouraged in that early in my life by dad. Our Twisleton forebears had walked the Yorkshire Dales from the 13th century. 'Twisleton' was then a hamlet on Whernside, with Ingleborough and Penyghent known as the 'Three Peaks'. Greg took me up Penyghent as a child as I came to take my sons David, John and James up years later. As Twisleton family genealogist I have written and given lectures on the family, notably Craven poet Tom Twisleton and his father, famous temperance campaigner Frank, affectionately known as 'The Craven Giant'. Greg gave me my middle name Fiennes to associate us with the southern branch of the family and my research put me in touch with them, notably Lord Saye and Sele at Broughton Castle and his celebrity cousin Captain Sir Ranulph Twisleton-Wykeham-Fiennes. (Appendix 1).

On arrival at Oxford in 1966 I encountered a fascinating, varied and creative culture with many opportunities to expand my horizons. With sights so well set within Chemistry my tutor and future research supervisor Australian John White well fostered my gifts. I attained the top first in Chemistry in 1969 and went on to be awarded a Senior Scholarship and then a Research Fellowship at St John's. My Doctorate was on the molecular dynamics of polythene and Teflon as examined by scattering neutron beams on samples of these polymers at Harwell's nuclear reactor. This work became part of a generation of research contributing to the emergence of light weight materials that can conduct electricity at room temperature, the components of today's phones and tablets. It was a pursuit of truth in which new horizons kept opening up. You felt drawn forward, motivated by something of an unveiling. What I helped discover was already there to be found. It was a matter of getting to the right place through the right theory and experimental work that confirmed the unveiling of those intermolecular force fields. As I use my smartphone a generation on I take pleasure in knowing my research and doctorate contributed with others to the materials and design of the circuit board serving its function. It's as if my seeking of the truth of things has come back to bless me.

As a scientist I see Christian faith as a form of wisdom going beyond but not against knowledge accessible to our minds. *How can I believe in a God I cannot see?* I made a well weighed decision. That is what faith is – a careful decision to act as if God were there and be energised by a power beyond oneself. Some things in life can't be tied down rationally. *God is one such thing*, and so is much of Chemistry. Contrary to popular perception, discovery of truth there relies on the subjective imagination of the scientist as well as the objective truth awaiting discovery. Both faith and reason lead us up to God, so Christian revelation is partner with and not rival to scientific knowledge, as the witness of so many believing scientists makes clear. As John Donne wrote 'Reason is our soul's left hand, faith his right, by these we reach divinity'.

In 1969 aged 21 I was heading on my Lambretta from Harwell up the A34 to my Oxford College when the front tyre burst and I went across the road to slide under a lorry. It was 29th September and I was heading to keep the Feast of St Michael & All Angels at my church of St Mary Magdalene in Oxford. The good news is I passed under the lorry though I missed that service and ended up in the Radcliffe Infirmary. I remain convinced St Michael and the angels were sent by God to protect my life for a purpose. A few years later that purpose was revealed. I left my work at Oxford University and the nuclear power station at Harwell to train as a priest. The angels who shifted the lorry, or my scooter, helped shift my career their way. I say 'their way' because angels and priests have the same mission: to bring God's love to people and people to God's love.

2   Artist in the making

I was born 1952 in Darlington, County Durham, the second daughter of Doris and Ervin Scott and by a twist of providence on my sister Kathleen's fifth birthday so 17 September is always a busy day in our family. I joined Kathleen at Reid Street School when I myself turned five, The Second World War (1939-1945) had turned our parents' expectations to thoughts of a better future for their offspring. My mother signed up for teacher training and my father joined an international club and began to teach himself German, learning shorthand and typing resulting in our hosting German friends and visiting acquaintances in that country. He left behind the manual work he had formerly toiled at. At Reid Street I thrived and enjoyed the schooling, passing the 11-plus, and going on to Grammar School. When I was 11 we moved from Darlington to Shipley, Yorkshire, where I attended The Salt Grammar School, making lifelong friendships, and passing GCSEs and A levels. My mother, having signed up for a teacher training course, began to ride her bike daily to college, loving the arts and crafts. Doris used her own daughters to practise on, which was the start of my lifelong interest and practice of sketching and painting. Her 3 year course ended successfully with the offer of a teaching post in Crossflatts Primary School and my father, who had gained qualifications at night school, was offered a job in Bradford Social Services, where he also thrived.

Dad didn't go to church. His faith had wavered during the war, when he had been posted to Palestine, and found "The Holy Land" he'd learned about in Sunday School was a place of conflict. Mum however took Kath and myself along to the local

Church. Larger and livelier than St Matthew's in Darlington, the new vicar of St Peter's, Shipley, Brandon Jackson, was stirring things up as he preached fiery evangelical sermons. People were coming to know Jesus, and the sense of commitment was strong. At 14 I began to go to the Youth Club. In order to attend you had to attend the Sunday Evening meeting, where the talks, films, testimonies and Bible Studies were challenging. I was amazed by girls my own age talking about an experience of meeting Jesus. One spoke of going to a Billy Graham rally. I didn't know who Billy Graham was – I thought it was a boxer or a footballer! She had taken her GCE study books with her to pass the time, but found herself listening to the talk, and, being compelled to go forward she gave her life to Jesus. It sounded terrifying, and when one of the leaders persuaded me to go to a gospel concert where there was an altar call, I sat there praying I wouldn't get that compulsion to get up out of my seat and make a fool of myself. Despite meaningful looks from the leader, I was relieved, and perhaps a bit disappointed when I emerged unscathed!

These born again Christians talked about praying – and getting answers! Of picking up a Bible and finding the words came alive – as though written personally for them. One said casually, "well, I had planned to be a teacher, but now I think God wants me to be a probation officer". My thoughts of God did not involve him personally interfering in my plans, or communicating with me. We had a Youth Fellowship week away at Capernwray, a Bible school, which was great fun, and I argued with my friends that I was a Christian – I'd always been a Christian. I thought maybe the girls who talked of a conversion experience came from homes where they hadn't been brought up to know about God. It must be nice to have such an experience, but I would never need that...

One night a few weeks later I went for a walk with another friend. As we walked in the dark and rain, we began to tell each other ghost stories and spooky things we'd overheard, and when the time came for us to go our separate ways, we were both terrified! As I ran home I felt overwhelmed by fear, and as though all the demons of hell were on my tail! I ran up to my bedroom and prayed for peace! I'd never feared death – everyone went to Heaven, didn't they? But now I thought, "what if I'm not a Christian?" But I am! I believe in You, God! What if I'm *not* saved?" One of the keen Christians had given me a booklet on John's Gospel, with daily readings, and I had it in my Bible, so I picked it up, still frantic with terror, still asking God to give me peace! I opened the booklet, and at the back was a prayer with the four steps to becoming a Christian. I baulked at that – I already *was* a Christian... and yet... I said, "Well, Lord, you know I'm already a Christian, I've always been one, but just to make absolutely sure I'm going to pray this prayer..." and so I did, telling God I believed in him, and his son Jesus who had died for the sins of the world. I admitted I was a sinner in need of salvation, and asked him to come into my heart. There! It was done - I'd signed the insurance policy, I was covered! And to my amazement all the fear was gone, and a tremendous peace was in its place

On leaving Salts Grammar School I was offered a job in Bradford, working in the local Art Gallery and Museum by day and attending evening classes to learn shorthand and typing. I also became a Sunday School teacher to 7 year olds, and enjoyed illustrating with my sketches the Bible stories I taught, along with more mature Christian women. I met Robert Cockerham (17) at the Mecca ballroom in Bradford. An apprentice engineer, tall, dark and handsome, he asked me to dance, and later escorted me to the bus stop and waited with me until the bus arrived. He said he would phone me... and... he did! "Would you like to come to the cinema?" "The Love Bug" was on at the local cinema, so we went to see the light hearted film, and then Robert walked me home. A light kiss and hug, and he set off for a lengthy walk home. We began to go out together and fell in love. I was reading a lot of Christian books, and I came across "In God's Underground" by Richard Wurmbrand, which talked about the persecution of Christians in Communist lands. I was stunned as I read about the torture being endured by my brothers and sisters, and deeply ashamed that my own faith cost me nothing at all. I was happy to be in church and youth fellowship, but at school I kept quiet about my Lord. If my friends knew I was a Christian, they didn't hear it from me! I fasted for the first time in my life, and repented of my shallowness, and asked God to take my whole life - I was his, I wanted to live for him. I felt him say, "If that's so, how can you be planning your life around Robert – he isn't a Christian". I had to put God first, and so I explained to a bewildered Rob what I felt God had told me. He was very hurt, and I felt miserable - it wasn't his fault, and I wasn't rejecting him, but it was a real shock that God meant so much to me, and he started to ask questions, which eventually after a few months led to him giving his own life to Christ. From then on we were more in love than ever, and with the added dimension of being able to pray together, go to Bible Studies and Prayer Groups together. He soon became a Sunday School teacher too, and we knew that eventually we would marry. Rob was doing a 7 year apprenticeship as a Post Office Telecommunications engineer.

3   A priestly calling

The leaf spoke and said 'Go and see Ken Noakes'. I was sitting in the College Gardens reading the paper after High Mass and something made me put down the paper and look up. Over at St Mary Magdalene's I'd been immersed in Anglocatholic worship and now my attention was diverted by the Sunday paper. The default setting of my unfocused mind was to be pondering the next stage of my Chemical research having been awarded a Sabbatical year in Denmark from my Research Fellowship at St John's. There I was in Oxford's most beautiful gardens, having a Sunday break from study, and something remarkable happened. I looked up at the tree beside the garden bench and became very alert. Something extraordinary was happening to me. I felt my attention drawn by the tree and as I looked at the young leaves it was as if one of them spoke to me. To this day how external to my mind that voice was I cannot fully recall but the subject of the communication was to go and see a priest I hardly knew called Ken Noakes who was based at Pusey House across the road from St John's. It was Sunday 20th May 1973 at 12.30pm and my life has never been the same since. I went across the road to Ken which started me on a process of abandoning my Chemistry to move fast track into the priesthood. By October that year having resigned my Fellowship and gained acceptance as ordinand by the Bishop of Oxford, I was at the College of the Resurrection, Mirfield. I had exchanged the 'ivory towers' of Oxford for the then 'satanic mills' of Huddersfield.

This call and change came as a surprise to me, my family, friends and colleagues. Besides its seeming supernatural origin I trace it back to the influence of my parents and school chaplain, Philip Curtis, who had pointed me gently towards Oxford's Anglocatholicism. The Vicar of St Mary Magdalene's, Oxford, Fr John Hooper had greatest influence upon me. Fr John was an old style charismatic priest who made God that much more real to me, so real I made my first Confession, discovered the awesome nature of the eucharist and the reality of the communion of saints, especially the Virgin Mary. I never looked back to Chemistry after my call though this academic formation came to play in my priestly ministry. At Oxford I made lifelong friends with Nigel Brown, Richard Catlow, John Connell, Gabriel De La Pena, Nick King, John Landais, Andrew Smyth and Hector Steen. I had one girl friend, Liz Abbot-Anderson and was close to Caroline Townsend and her family but left Oxford unattached.

Leaving Oxford I went for the first year of my priestly training to the Hostel of the Resurrection in Leeds and then for two years at the College of the Resurrection at Mirfield. Over this period I spent vacations in Giggleswick and was present at my dad Greg's death aged 73 on Friday 19 April 1974 following a debilitating stroke. The priest at Holy Ascension, Settle, Canon Eric Ashby took dad's funeral and was an inspiration to me, by then a server at Settle Church. My friend Roger Miller's dad, Canon Edward Miller at Giggleswick was another clerical influence, as was St John's College Chaplain, Eric Heaton. Among the Community of the Resurrection monks Benedict Green, Denys Lloyd and Cedma Mack were influential as was a lay friend, John Teasdale. As I trained I made close friendships with John Beynon, Derek Jay, Paul Newman, Tony Perry and Mark Thomas.

The Company of Mission Priests (CMP) run clergy houses in challenging mainly urban parishes and I joined their house at SS Philip & James, New Bentley in my native Doncaster with Fr Roy Pannell being ordained priest 3rd July 1977 in Sheffield Cathedral. In CMP you made an annual promise to stay single to be free for service. In my Curacy at Bentley I also had an experience of renewal in the Holy Spirit through a faith crisis which took me back to Mirfield. I believe God has a sense of humour. I know he is always telling me to 'take a leaf out of my book' because after I followed his first invitation he put me straight 5 years later in September 1978 through another leaf on another tree as I describe in my book 'Meet Jesus' (Appendix 2):

'Shortly after I was ordained priest... I had a real crisis of faith. I went back on a sort of retreat to the Community of the Resurrection at Mirfield where I had trained. It was a chance to work out what should happen next since I hardly believed in the reality of God anymore. While there I was taken under the wing of Fr. Daniel, one of the monks of the Community. He gave me this advice: 'Maybe, John, it is not Jesus who's gone but your vision of him. Why not pray an honest prayer, like, 'Lord, if you're there, show yourself. Give me a vision of yourself that's to your dimensions and not mine'. With nothing to lose I prayed Fr Daniel's prayer and waited for probably the most difficult and cliff-hanging two days of my life. Then Jesus answered. He chose a leaf on a tree in the monastery garden. I was walking along with no particular thought in my head when my eyes fell on the leaf – and it was as if it spoke to me. 'He made you', the leaf seemed to say. I was bowled over. As I moved forward I saw the great Crucifix that stands in the rockery. 'I made you. I love you', the figure of Jesus seemed to say. 'Father, Son... what about the Holy Spirit?', my mind was spinning. The Father was saying 'I made you', the Son 'I love you'. Could it be that the Spirit was saying 'I want to fill you'? A group of Mirfield Fathers prayed for me to be filled afresh with the Holy Spirit - and from that day forward Jesus has seemed much closer to me, in his word as well as sacrament, in people and nature as well as in church' pp42-43.

During my Curacy I was involved with Fr Pannell in caring for the families bereaved by the Bentley Colliery paddy train crash of 1978 which killed our CMP housekeeper Eunice's husband Jim Mitchell and six other miners, bringing me direct contact with miners' leader Arthur Scargill. Scargill was to further impact me after I moved in 1978 to be parish priest of St Wilfrith, Moorends, Doncaster serving through the 1984-5 mining dispute and writing a parish history, 'Moorends and its Church' (See Appendix 2). Over my 7 years at Moorends the congregation doubled as priest and people weathered the dispute. Back to live near Thorne I picked up again with our family links with the Oglesby family, John especially. Whilst at Moorends I had regular visits from my Settle-based mother Elsie. Both of us were deeply grieved at the tragic death of my brother Tony in São Paulo, Brazil on 19th March 1984.

The most chilling aspect of Tony's suicide was the receipt for the gas cylinder and large plastic bag purchased two months before he used them to end his life. Though his death was swift and painless, planning it for weeks in advance revealed his depth of despair. As manager of a failing theatre costume company in São Paulo, Brazil, he seems to have decided that the day he could not pay his workers would be his last. Neither my mother or I had picked up the gravity of his financial crisis in regular phone calls so when his bank manager phoned me to say he had committed suicide I could not at first believe it. It was the saddest day of my life bringing me responsibility to break the news of my brother's death to our widowed mother. To lose your only sibling at 33 years takes away one who helps recall from nearest to your perspective your childhood, adolescence and early career. Like many brothers with a two year gap we were in competition. Tony was more charismatic with a wider circle of friends. He was less focussed and sat more lightly to religious adherence. As such he was a great foil, challenging and sharpening my thinking, helping me to see it's in giving out that we receive and build friendships. The suffering was like losing a limb and initially threw my life out of balance. It brought full responsibility for my ageing mother's welfare. Bereavement through suicide has such sharpness with the painful haunting question: 'if, only...'. Could I have phoned him more? Of course I could, though what difference it would have made is another question. So many of his peers, girlfriend included, were as astonished by Tony's suicide as we were.

The death of a loved one deliberately, without notice and in a fashion seemingly forgetful of those they leave behind, especially their widowed mother, is galling. Only as fuller circumstances of Tony's death emerged over the weeks that followed did I build forgiveness towards him. The clinical planning of his suicide evidenced deep isolation despite his having a business partner who could have taken more financial responsibility if he had been alerted. Anger at a bereavement such as this was and still is on occasion, along with my lamenting Anne's Alzheimer's, directed against the universe and God for allowing such a tragedy and the accompanying grief and suffering. At the same time it was and is the taking of an eternal perspective to Tony's death that has eased suffering over the years besides helping me sympathise with others who have suffered the suicide of a loved one. In suffering bereavement we rediscover our humanity as John Donne captures famously: 'Any man's death diminishes me... I am involved in mankind... never send to know for whom the bell tolls; it tolls for thee.' Elsie's Hellifield-based mother, Eliza, died a year after Tony. My grandma had always been a formative influence upon Tony and I. Elsie's brother John Vickers, married to Doreen, was another inspiration and I have kept up with their children, my cousins Helen and Paul and their families.

CMP had members in the former British colony of Guyana, South America. In 1986 one of these, Canon John Dorman wrote to me out of the blue saying it was at the Holy Spirit's prompting to plead for him to consider helping train a group of Amerindians to be priests. I was consequently invited by the Bishop of Guyana, Randolph George to be Principal of the Alan Knight Training Centre in Guyana's interior with the sponsorship of USPG (then 'United Society for the Propagation of the Gospel' now 'United Society Partners in the Gospel'). My acceptance of that call, which was to change my life in so many ways, was with my widowed and recently bereaved mother Elsie's generous support. In autumn 1986 I began six months orientation at USPG's College of Ascension in Selly Oak, Birmingham with another UK based CMP friend, Fr Allan Buik.

John Twisleton with Elsie Twisleton 1949

Elsie, John, Tony and Greg Twisleton c1960

Greg Twisleton in Catteral Hall father's race around 1960

John Twisleton at Giggleswick School speech day 1966

John Twisleton rowing no 5 for one of St John's College, Oxford eights around 1968

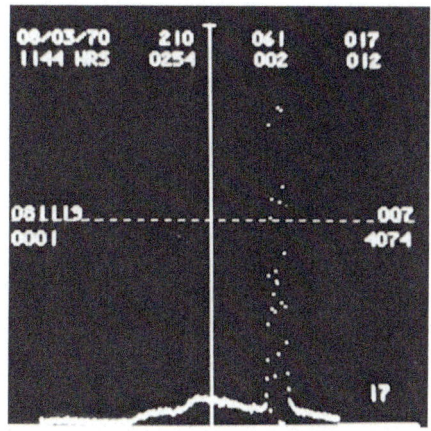

Inelastic neutron scattering spectrum from Harwell used in John Twisleton's polymer dynamics doctoral thesis 1973

John's Chemistry tutor Dr John White around 1966

John's parish priest Fr John Hooper around 1970

Canon Eric Ashby, Fr Peter Yates, Fr Roy Pannell & Alan Parkinson at Fr John Twisleton's First Mass in SS Philip & James, New Bentley, Doncaster 4 July 1977

Street evangelism in Moorends, Doncaster 1980s

Anne Scott, Doris Scott, Kath Scott & Ethel Lumley 1952

Anne and Kath Scott around 1955

Marriage of Anne Scott and Robert Cockerham 1973

Anne, David, John & Robert Cockerham about 1980

Robert Cockerham at HCJB Radio in Ecuador c1978

Burial of Robert Cockerham in Quito 1981

Robertpsalm

Today you were swept under the sea
And only your lifeless frame came back again.
The word just came
As merrily we rowed along
With only life in view
Until tonight.

No details yet.
Just a brief telephone message
And a desperate hope that someone's wrong.
In a moment
All our wives became widows
And all our children became orphans,
And sleep scoffs
As a million moving pictures tell us
How it must have been.

Lean, tall, gentle Robert,
Is that vigorous youthful face really over there tonight
Being given a royal welcome by His Majesty?
Is Anne really staring at a half-empty bed . . . .
Or trying to explain to the boys about eternity?

Lift her up, Father.
We're too far away tonight,
But You're there.
Please hold her in Your mighty arms
And don't let her go until she and they are safely with You, too.

A mystery it's always been
Why choicest fruit is often plucked still green,
And why it takes a mighty wave of shock
To drive us from our boats,
Where merrily we rowed along
With only life in view,
Into a glimpse of the glorious urgent now,
And into a determination to redeem that now
Before our wave falls heavy too.

A moment to weep . . . .
Then out to the battle again.
A world's to be won,
And other waves are crashing down
On swimmers less prepared for doom.

Thank you, Robert.
We could not rescue you from death,
So you rescued us from sloth.
Oh, may today's sting not fade
Until the Spirit's work is done in us
And through us in His glorious plan
And our glorious task.

David Cliffe

10th February, 1981 (used by permission of the poet)

33

4   Missionaries

Robert Cockerham and I were married in 1973 and set up home in Shipley, not far from both sets of parents, and our church and life was good! A year or so later our church had a huge emphasis on overseas mission, with lots of invited speakers, meals, prayer. Two of the speakers were from a Radio station we'd heard of as part of the missionary prayer group - Radio HCJB (Heralding Christ Jesus' Blessings), which broadcast all over the world from Quito in Ecuador. With Rob's interest in Radio, and my passion for reaching into the Communist world, we were fascinated by George and Margaret Poole and what they had to say. As we drove home after the talk, Rob was thoughtful. George was an engineer, working with the sophisticated satellites and antennas and transmitters required for sending out programmes in (at that time) 15 languages to most parts of the world. "I could do that job!" he said. And Margaret was, like me, a secretary. A year later, after many letters and forms and interviews we went to Bible College as the next step in our application to the World Radio Missionary Fellowship. We didn't go alone – our first son, David, was 7 weeks old. After a year at Capernwray, and then a deputation tour when we went to churches all over the country to speak about the work of Radio HCJB and encourage supporters, and with the financial and prayer backing of our Church and family, we went to Costa Rica to learn Spanish at a missionary language school for two terms, and arrived in Ecuador in September 1977. Our second son, John, was born 3 months later.

Robert fitted right into the engineering team, his training and qualifications being well up to the demands of the work at the transmitter site, where 6 engineering families were situated, well outside the capital city of Quito. The transmitters and one of the two hospitals were based there, and most of the 200 missionaries lived and worked there. It was a wonderful community, a family - many languages and from different countries, with skills ranging across technical, medical, teaching, musical, pastoral, writers and from many different church denominations. We didn't worry about doctrinal or liturgical styles - we had one statement of faith and were bound together in the unity of bringing the good news of Jesus Christ to our radio listeners and to the people around us in Ecuador.

In our second term as missionaries, in 1981, my Dad came out to visit us. We borrowed the station pick up, packed things up, and drove the 6 hours from the heights of the Andes mountains down steep and perilous roads to the heat of the jungles and the beach at Atacames. We were all in high spirits and looking forward to a break. Rob did all the driving, so he had a sleep in the cabin we had rented while the boys, Dad and I went onto the beach and played in the sand and the sea. Later, I made an evening meal, then Dad sat on the beach with the boys paddling in the shallows and Rob and I went for a swim. The tide was going out, and I found myself struggling in a strong wave, being turned over and over and unable to find the sand under my feet. As I fought for control, I heard Rob shouting for help. Dad hadn't noticed, and I knew I couldn't help Rob when I was in trouble myself, so I shouted and waved as I swam and finally reached the shore. Dad, meanwhile, had seen Rob's difficulties and he dived into the water and swam towards him. He wasn't able to get past that huge rolling wave, and he saw Rob disappear. I tried to find help, but the beach was deserted, and by the time anyone heard my shouts and came to see what was happening, it was too late. Kneeling on the sand with David and John, I told them that we must pray. I thanked God for his constant love and presence, and that Robert belonged to him, and had no fear of death. I thanked him for the certainty of Heaven for those who trust in him, and asked him to take care of me and the boys as we faced life without our wonderful husband and father. Robert's body came back, and of course we tried CPR but he was dead. So this much loved husband, father and friend was taken home to Heaven, and at 28 years old I was a widow.

The funeral in the English Church most of the missionaries in Quito attended was full of faith and the gospel was preached to the large congregation, mostly missionaries but also local workers employed by the station, men Rob had worked with, friends we'd met. Two people answered a call to give their lives to Christ. I helped our friend Geoff Roberts create a testimonial to Rob in 'Mightier than the Waves' (Appendix 2). After a brief return to Britain to deal with insurances and legal matters and be comforted by our family and friends, I returned to Ecuador as a missionary but two years later as John approached school age, the Lord showed me it was time to return to the UK. I was a single parent, with very little money, and life was tough. I prayed for a husband. At the start of 1986 I felt the Lord saying, "The boys are old enough now for you to look towards a future career". I'd been doing all kinds of odds and ends to make ends meet and still look after the boys – temping, working part time in offices and a bakery, having lodgers, typing out theses for students at Bradford University and writing. I threw myself into pushing doors to see which ones would open, praying for guidance and further insight. I went to interviews, some of which I didn't succeed in, others I closed the door on, looked into computer training and went to a missionary conference. Two of my prayer partners showed me an ad in the Church Times – the Bishop of Argentina needed a Diocesan Administrator – an Anglican, Spanish speaker, secretarial skills needed. I said to 10 year old David, "what do you think?" "Well, I don't know why, but I think it might be right!" he replied. That was exactly how I felt, and so I took the next step of contacting USPG, the missionary society who would fund the post and deal with the travel and accommodation arrangements of the person appointed. The process continued and after being invited I set about the required 6 months missionary training USPG put its workers through at the then College of Ascension Selly Oak in Birmingham.

David and John roamed around the college building as I unpacked, met up with, and introduced me to "Father" John Twisleton, who had worked in mining parishes in South Yorkshire, and as well as being further up the ecclesiastical candle than the other priests, he had led his parishes into the charismatic experience. We became friends, and as he was on his way to Guyana to live in the jungle and train 12 Amerindian men for 3 years to be Anglican priests, and as he was dedicated to a life of celibacy as a priest, he seemed a "safe" person to befriend. Less than 3 weeks after meeting, John proposed to me! I turned him down without a thought, but he asked me if I would pray about it. When I did, I felt God making me re-examine all the qualities I was looking for in a life partner. I had a list of essential qualities in a husband – Christian, (preferably charismatic), someone willing to serve God abroad, who would get on well with my sons, good natured... the list had been added to over the 7 years of my widowhood. John fitted most of the criterion but I said to God, "I never expected an Anglocatholic!!" I hadn't thought to put that on my list!

5   Marriage in Guyana

The seminary for Amerindian ordinands in Guyana's interior was fitting memorial to the 42 year service of Alan Knight (1904-1979), Bishop of Guyana from 1937 until his death whose robust Anglocatholicism drew a succession of missionaries from the Church of England to South America. Knight's episcopacy paralleled in stature and length that of Bishop William Austin (1807-1892) and preceded the long reign of his Guyanese successor Bishop Randolph George (1924-2016). Through partnership primarily with the Company of Mission Priests (CMP) and USPG eighteen Amerindian priests were trained initially through the Alan Knight Training Centre at Yupukari, Knight's memorial seminary. One of its trainees, Fr Alfred David, was ordained further as a Bishop in 2021. This consecration was applauded at the last meeting of the 90 year old Guyana Diocesan Association (GDA) in June 2021 capturing something of the fruit of missionary enterprise from the Church of England tracing back to 1781.

This précis history of Guyana at the back of GDA's September 1968 magazine possibly written by Alan Knight himself captures this extraordinary land which drew so many missionaries: 'The country lies on the north-east coast of the South American continent, between Venezuela on the west, Surinam on the east, with the Atlantic Ocean facing it on the north. It is as large as the combined areas of England, Scotland and Wales... It has pleasant climatic conditions for the greater part of the year. It is particularly so on the coastal area where it is sub-tropical. Columbus sailed along the Guyana coast in 1498, and later wrote about the great rivers of Guyana flowing down from an earthly paradise... Sir Walter Raleigh voyaged to the country in 1595. The task of shaping Guyana's history was shared among the Dutch, French and British. Between 1841 and 1931 some 433,643 immigrants arrived in Guyana on the basis of an indentureship system... serving agriculture (coconuts, rice, coffee and limes in addition to sugar)... Wherever shouts of "Gold! Gold!" were raised, history provides evidence of men flocking thither. Guyana has not been the exceptional case'.

I wear a wedding ring made with Guyana gold blessed on Pentecost Sunday 1988 in St Mary, Yupukari where, whilst serving as second AKTC Principal, I was married to Anne by our Amerindian parish priest Fr Edwin Rogers. The parish of Guyana's Rupununi near the Brazilian border has in fact long association with the lost city of gold known as El Dorado. Our journey to Guyana started with my friendship with Canon John Dorman (1916-1998) who wrote to me in 1985 with typical spiritual force asking me to consider crossing the Atlantic to train as priest candidates selected by Bishop George and his team. It was hard to say no to this 'English Saint', founder member of CMP, considered now as suitable for inclusion in the Calendar of the Church in the Province of the West Indies. Canon Dorman's advocacy for Guyana's Amerindians, faced with the challenge of integration with Guyanese society as a whole, was courageous, helping them challenge mining and logging ventures damaging their livelihood.

We started married life in a mud brick house at Yupukari with no phone, monthly mail and a book called 'Where there is no doctor'. David returned to the UK to Anne's parents Ervin and Doris in Shipley for school but little John received education with the Amerindian village children. In running the seminary John was assisted by Fr Allan Buik CMP and Anne also helped, especially in building Christian fellowship among the ordinands' wives. The parish had a Ranch so John had responsibility for 200 cows and a team of vaqueros as well as for providing for the ordinands and their families, a community of almost 100 to start with, that were frequently short of food. Yupukari was a remote location where hunting and fishing took second place to worship, teaching and pastoral outreach in the Rupununi region of Guyana. Anne describes conditions there at the time in 'Guyana Venture' (Appendix 2):

'All our water was brought from the river a mile away, and as gas was expensive, we did not boil it, but drank it, amoebas and all. The whole village went down to the river to bathe each evening, and to wash their clothes on convenient rocks, trying to avoid the sting rays, alligators, piranhas and other creatures in the black water, such as anacondas and giant otters. Bats roosted in the rafters of the vicarage and Allan's house - only the mosquito nets shielded us (more or less) from their droppings. Snakes were common. They were all assumed to be poisonous and the locals would dispatch them with their machetes. Sometimes a jaguar's footprints would be spotted, and on one occasion a dog, sleeping on a doorstep, was taken in the night. Allan was shaving one morning when a small snake popped its head through the overflow. On another occasion, as the students came for the very early service at the church, they all dipped their fingers in the holy water and crossed themselves. When it got lighter, a small snake was seen to be swimming happily in the stoop. Every day or two we inspected our feet and used a needle to dig out jiggers, which if not noticed would lay their eggs under our skin. The Amerindians travelled mainly on the river in dug out canoes to tend their farms, and to spear fish as they went. Bows and arrows were used to catch monkeys, wild pigs, and other creatures at night. An iguana might be the catch of the day, chopped up, intestines and all, and served up in a stew. And yes, it was as revolting as it sounds!' pp 75-76.

The work of training priests at Yupukari kept us aware of the Amerindian culture we inhabited. The forest people of Guyana believe in many evil spirits, above all what they call 'kenaima'. A youth around 18 was fishing one day and felt kenaima attack him from behind. The evil spirit is said to go up the rectum. Whether it was a physical attack by the demon or psychological we do not know. What we know is that when we came to his hammock the life was literally ebbing away from him and his family were planning where his grave should be. To be attacked by kenaima was a death sentence without respite in the old village religion. Praise God for the new religion and for the triumphant power of Christ in the Blessed Sacrament! We encouraged the youth as we prepared him for the Sacrament of Anointing and Holy Communion in words adapted from St. John's first letter 4:4: 'The one who is in you is greater than the one who is in the world': Jesus in you is greater than kenaima! Most of the village gathered into Church and the Blessed Sacrament was exposed for a prayer vigil for the boy during which a priest took Holy Communion to him. A vigil of prayer and praise to God continued all night as the boy's strength returned. The next Sunday he was with the Music group playing the guitar at Mass. His seizing upon the triumphant power of Christ, especially present in Holy Communion, which brings the power and presence of Jesus deep into us, saved his life.

We lived two years at Yupukari, Fr John three in total, engaging in an unfamiliar age-old culture built, as many indigenous people still are, around the cooking pot and the daily quest for food to cook and firewood to cook it with. Because the students had, in order, daily Mattins, Mass, Meditation, Lectures, Seminars and Evensong there proved to be insufficient time for hunting and fishing. This meant hunger at times - even days of prayer for food - and in answer to prayer on occasion Diocesan provision of sacks of rice, flour and sugar flown in by plane at great cost. Our small family was blessed to have a lot of time for one another centring on the daily evening walk down to the Rupununi river to bathe with the other villagers. Our day ended with star gazing, a great gift with the unpolluted skies, and listening to the BBC World Service. The ordination of six men as priests by Bishop Randolph on 23rd April 1990 released us to return briefly to Anne's native Shipley.

6   Sent to Coventry

We were 'sent to Coventry' in 1990
a good term, at first, and nothing alien
spending six years in a vibrant city
out in the suburb of Holbrooks
as a family just made five
by the birth of Anthony James.

Our sending we thought came from God
through the invitation of Bishop Simon
to further grow Saint Luke's Church
in faith, love and numbers
following 39 years of Father Henry
a legend in the land!

Fr John set to work visiting,
James often in his backpack.
Anne made the Vicarage home
studying, drawing and painting.
David to Bluecoat and University,
John to Cardinal Newman.

What a privilege to live in a city
after years in the forest of Guyana!
A city like Christ, dying then rising,
with bombed ruins beside a new Cathedral,
image of forgiveness extended to all
through the Coventry cross of nails.

At St Luke's the Anglocatholic vision
became a Cross through being set apart
from mainstream Church of England
by the ordination of women priests,
the need to rejoice with the rejoicing
and mourn loss of Catholic vision.

This was John's true 'sending to Coventry'
with Anne carrying much of his pain,
assuaged by the joy of toddler James
as both Church and family grew up,
confused by Christian divisions,
yet finding gain through pain.

One gain was moving to a house
on the slopes of Alexandra Palace and
a London mission role with Bishop Brian.
We headed south with James and John,
and new work for John, Anne and David,
starting a new chapter of life together.

John Twisleton   11 July 2023

My poem captures something of the roller coaster of our six years at St Luke's Church, Holbrooks in Coventry. On our return from Guyana after the ordinations consequent to AKTC we lived in Anne's house in Shipley. From April to December 1990 I was unemployed which was a benefit for us with Anne's pregnancy and our family reuniting itself with David (15), my mother Elsie in Settle and Anne's parents Ervin and Doris down the road. They had stood 2 years in loco parentis for David. We were also reunited with Anne's sister Kath, her husband Brian and our nieces Clare, Emma and Sarah. Over our time in Shipley Anne reconnected with St Peter's, her sending Church when she and Rob went to Ecuador, and I with the Anglocatholic parish of St Chad, Toller Lane with its saintly incumbent, Fr Ralph Crowe SSC who became a lifelong friend. I applied for jobs across the Church of England and a conversation with the Bishop of Coventry, Simon Barrington-Ward about St Luke's Church, Holbrooks proved conclusive. Anthony James was born in September 1990, as David had been before, in Bradford Infirmary and the adoption of David and John was later agreed and finalised 1992. With baby James in tow we moved just before Christmas in a snowstorm to St Luke's Vicarage in the multicultural suburb of Coventry called Holbrooks which sits on the secret of its name. The 'brooks' criss crossing the suburb are now held in culverts. Holbrooks marking the northern boundary of Coventry is adjacent to junction 3 of the M6 handy for visiting parents in Settle and Shipley as well as friends in London. Our new congregation had a large contingent of West Indian origin and the suburb a strong Asian community, primarily, Sikh, which made Holbrooks home from home after life in multicultural Guyana.

Basilica-style St Luke's Church, red brick with an external altar and pulpit, was designed by N.F. Cashmaille-Day, built 1939 and bombed the next year. The air raid on Coventry on the night of 14 November 1940 was the single most concentrated attack on a British city in the Second World War. The Luftwaffe dropped 500 tons of high explosive, 30,000 incendiaries and 50 landmines. Following the raid, seemingly in revenge for the RAF bombing of Munich, Nazi propagandists coined a new word in German - 'coventrieren' - to raze a city to the ground. This action was legitimised in warfare terms given Coventry's hosting of metal and wood-working industries producing cars, bicycles, aeroplane engines and munitions. St Luke's suffered repairable damage reopening about 1950 in contrast to St Michael's Cathedral which was completely destroyed, rebuilt and reconsecrated 1962. After the Cathedral burned down in 1940 so-called Coventry Crosses of Nails made from large nails found in the ashes were distributed worldwide focusing a ministry of reconciliation linked to the death and resurrection of the Cathedral mirroring that of Christ. The current Archbishop of Canterbury Justin Welby served on the reconciliation team.

Reconciliation was a key theme in the ministry of Coventry's Bishop Simon Barrington-Ward. Both of us supported and encouraged St Luke's to support a monthly Sunday evening get together that he convened of churches across denominations with a charismatic flavour including testimonies and the ministry of prayer with laying on of hands. Our parish contained Coventry's largest Roman Catholic Church of the Holy Family who in the same spirit partnered St Luke's with the African Methodist Episcopal Church in an ecumenical mission 'Mission Holbrooks' of 1992 including a big 'March for Jesus'. That same year St Luke's had its own reconciliation challenge as the General Synod voted to ordain women priests. Anglocatholic parishes look to the faith and practice of the universal church, Roman Catholic and Orthodox, who maintain a male priesthood, seeing the priest as a symbol of Jesus not to be dislocated. John helped lead the parish into Forward in Faith, the dissenting Church of England body, now The Society, maintaining Catholic order. With a small group at St Luke's ready to accept women priests Anne was made to feel beleaguered especially as some friends changed churches as a result of this church council resolution. We did our best to rejoice with the rejoicing and mourn with the mourners on this issue but it was difficult and tipped me towards depression, again hard for Anne. Both of us thankfully had domestic joys to compensate us for the challenges next door in St Luke's with toddler James and our two eager babysitters, David and John. In Coventry David attended Blue Coat Church School, John went to Cardinal Newman Roman Catholic School and James eventually to Parkgate Primary School. Besides being a homemaker Anne followed a part-time degree course in Arts and Crafts at Coventry University, helped by some rescheduling by John, to develop her sketching and painting. Our parents, Elsie, Ervin and Doris were regular visitors driving down from Yorkshire. John was active in St Luke's scouts and David, when a student at Brighton then Nottingham University, served behind the bar at Hen Lane Club, the social hub for many parishioners. As a priest in Doncaster, Coventry, London and Sussex my social outreach, besides visiting homes, has always been in such formerly named 'working men's clubs'. In my early years of home visiting around Holbrooks I was often accompanied by James in his baby backpack, a winning feature right up to the end of 'the terrible twos' when ornaments were put at risk!

During our last years at St Luke's Anne, with Roman Catholic friends, contributed to successful Life in the Spirit seminars, the original Alpha Course, at St Luke's. I headed up a welcome church project linking structural alterations to make St Luke's more physically welcome to spiritual renewal to gain more of 'the welcoming love of Christ in our hearts'. Whilst on 3 months Sabbatical Leave in Guyana 1995, with a brief to encourage the Amerindian ministries we had helped form, John delivered 15 tea chests of books, toys and baby clothes collected by the parish for the work of the Mother's Union. A team worked with John on a well received 'Holbrooks History' published coincident with the news we were leaving for London and a diocesan mission role without parish responsibilities. The Archdeacon of Coventry, Ian Russell, relayed to us in a letter written November 1996 his and the congregation's appreciation of both our ministries:

'Last night's Section 12 meeting at St Luke's revealed again the very real spiritual and special ministry you both exercised there. You really turned the place "inside out" so that the strong focus of eucharistic worship became the springboard to outreach, evangelism and service in and to the community. We thank God for all that you both were and did, in that church and congregation, deanery and in the city. I realise it was often hard for both of you, albeit in different ways, and your Christian joy and commitment were examples to us all'.

7   London calling

Journeying together we have moved at regular intervals linked to John's church appointments. The move from Coventry opened up new possibilities for me since parish attachment was of my choice. When John became Missioner for the Edmonton Area of London in 1996 we moved to a beautiful vicarage on the slopes of Alexandra Palace and I attended St James's, Muswell Hill. There I became very involved in 'The Big Lunch', a Christian club a group of parents started in the school James attended, and eventually became a Churchwarden. I joined a Bible study, and when a Peruvian Pastor and family fetched up at St James's, eager to work among the many Hispanics in London, I helped them set up a Spanish Church at St. James's. I did translation as the Cuevas spoke poor English, helped them as they approached schools and found housing, and took my turn preaching along with another man who also spoke Spanish. Building on enabling work I did in Coventry with young people I found employment with Volunteer Reading Help training in the end 30 plus volunteers to help reading in over 20 schools in Haringey. A highlight of our time in London was a three week visit to Peru in 1999, with a team of eight from St James's. We visited the home church of the Cuevas whose Spanish ministry I was part of. What a thrill to be back in the Andes mountains, and to be plunged into the life of a vibrant and dedicated group of believers! Though only two of the team spoke fluent Spanish, all of us were taken out onto the streets to sing and play, present storyboard talks, and then speak one to one with the crowds who stopped to listen to these strange 'gringos'. We were a very mixed bunch of people, but experienced a marvellous unity and family spirit both as a team and with our generous hosts in Lima, Huancayo and Cerro de Pasco, and we saw God's Spirit working powerfully for each of us, in the church and with the people we met and spoke to about Jesus. If it hadn't been for missing the family, I could happily have stayed!

In Doncaster my parish ministry gave me experience of dramatic Church growth linked to the prioritisation of intercessory prayer, as well as experience of working across the divide in the mining dispute. In Guyana with USPG I taught the Faith in a college where English was the second language for many of the ordinands, which made me more aware of our need to be clear about the Faith and 'put it simple'. My time in Coventry, in a parish with a large Sikh population, schooled me in inter-faith dialogue which was an important equipping for the work in North London. The then predominantly Anglocatholic Edmonton Area of London Diocese had been much affected by the 1992 decision to ordain women to the priesthood. I encountered and countered a lot of cynicism about the future of the Church of England. Our joint experience of charismatic renewal alongside Anne's Anglican Evangelical tradition helped this work. We often say our marriage costs a lot here but is also worth a lot. Networking across Christian traditions is natural to us. The future of the Church of England is ecumenical if it is anything at all - part of the Church *in* England. Ecclesiology became one of my areas of theological interest as well as spiritual ecumenism.

In London and later in Chichester Diocese I found myself promoting a theme of 'Being the Church Better' counter to the more radical and controversial 'Reshaping the Church' themes around in mission circles. Church revitalisation seems more about the deepening, refreshing and renewal of faith rather than a 'dreaming of systems so perfect that no one will need to be good' (Eliot). This tallied with the views of my appointing Bishop, Brian Masters. As his Missioner in the Edmonton Area of London Diocese my task was to work with parishes in evangelism whilst helping focus and develop the Area's overall mission strategy. In practice this involved me in weeks, fortnights or months seconded to parishes. Negotiating best use of my time between Bishop Brian, his Area Deans and the incumbents of our 100 parishes, I involved myself in parish missions, weeks of rededication, guided prayer weeks; training in the healing ministry and devising open air witnesses. I was instrumental in establishing an annual evangelistic 'Magnificat' Youth Weekend and a Weekend on The Church's Healing Ministry. In 1999 I helped head up 'The Edmonton Walk', a venture in prayer, encouragement and outreach beating the bounds of the boroughs of Barnet, Camden, Enfield and Haringey supported by 80% of parishes. This culminated in an Edmonton Area Eucharist up the road from our house inside Alexandra Palace at Pentecost and a walk from London to the Shrine of Our Lady in Walsingham for which James joined me. I was also involved in promoting the Chichester Diocesan renewal programme 'Fan the Flame' in the London Diocese. It was a privilege to be a member of the colourful Area Bishop's Staff monthly meeting which started around his conference table and ended with a glass or two of wine around a lunch table down the road in a Camden restaurant. Bishop Brian's untimely death in 1998 and the appointment of a new Bishop - my friend Peter Wheatley - made it appropriate to begin to look around again for what Our Lord may have in store for me as a priest, teacher and evangelist and a move best suited to the family.

'London Calling' was the call sign for the BBC World Service, dear to us over our years in Guyana, at one time to enemy occupied territory during the Second World War. Radio broadcasting brought Anne and Rob to Ecuador. This chapter heading for Anne and my journey together, 'London calling', connects with our call south from Coventry but it has a second connection with my involvement just after its 1995 creation up to today with London based Premier Christian Radio. This came at the invitation of presenters Cindy Kent and Justin Brierley. Justin invited me to bring in our atheist friend and London neighbour Clive Boutle to start the world famous 'Unbelievable' series engaging Christians with those of different worldviews. Premier broadcasts 24 hours a day offering a wide and varied range of entertaining and informative programming based on the beliefs and values of the Christian faith. The major emphasis is on news, current concerns and lifestyle issues and there are also programmes that explain and commend Christian belief. Praise and worship songs and traditional, modern and classic hymns and music are mixed together to create a unique sound. In a practical way Premier also responds to its listening audience through Lifeline, its telephone helpline service. I am a regular contributor to Premier and have helped produce a number of resources to help build Christian faith linked to my different radio series. More in Appendix 2 and at www.premierchristianradio.com.

As our time in London drew to a close in 2000 we went to Guyana with James (10) for a tour revisiting old haunts including St Mary, Yupukari where we renewed our marriage vows. After Anne and James returned to London I went to visit Fr Allan Alfred (now known as Carter) at Issano, a remote location in the jungle on the Mazaruni River where I had the shock of being bitten by a vampire bat. I awoke at 1am in the morning to hear the whirring of wings and to find my foot in a pool of blood! Determined not to be a preacher who foamed at the mouth I took a precautionary rabies injection! I survived and the experience helped break the ice at my interview with the Bishop of Chichester, Eric Kemp in Hove on my return a week or two later when he asked me what I had been busy with recently. I was offered the post of Chichester Diocesan Adviser for Mission and Renewal on 14 December 2000.

It was a wrench to leave David, now courting Denise Ward, and John, both employed in London as well as St James's Church family after such a fulfilling few years for both of us. Anne was less bereaved of London than Fr John, writing to friends 'What I *won't* miss about London is the horrendous traffic, and the desperate hunt for a place to park. A quieter, gentler pace near the beautiful South Downs is an attractive proposition'.

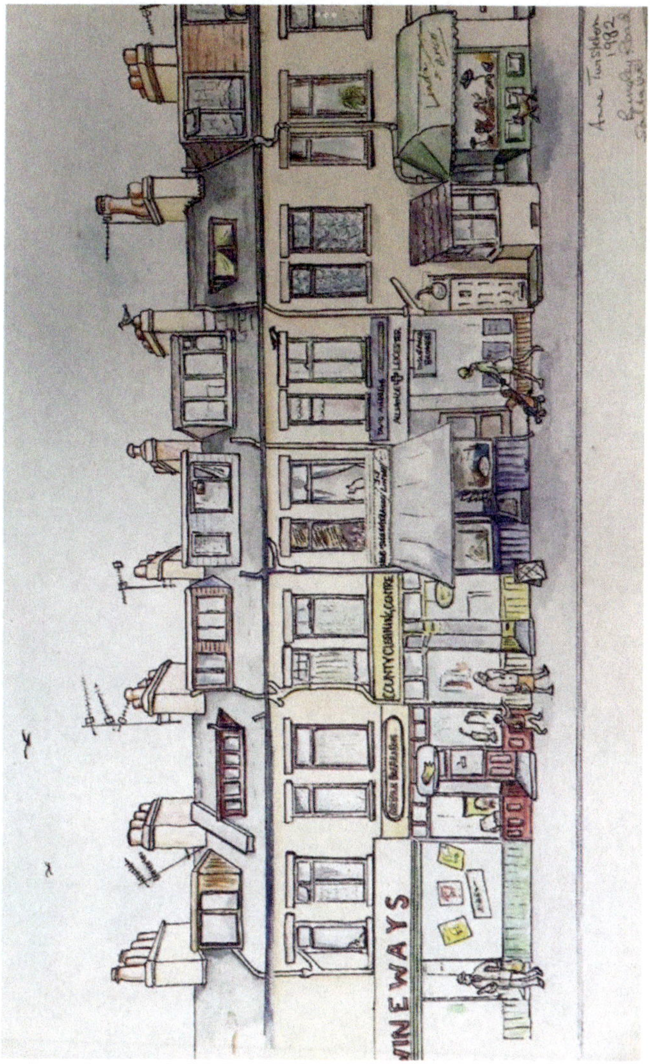
WINEWAYS

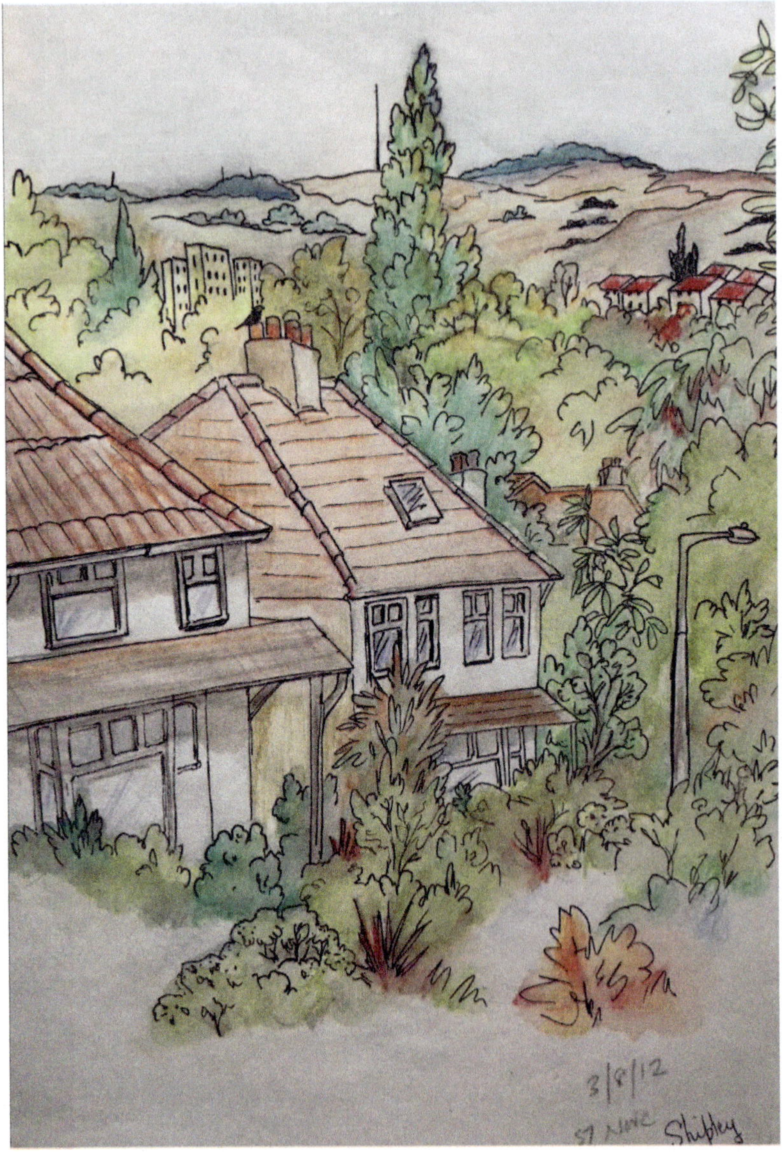
3/8/12
Shipley

Capernwray Reunion with Billy Strachan in London

Billy Strachan

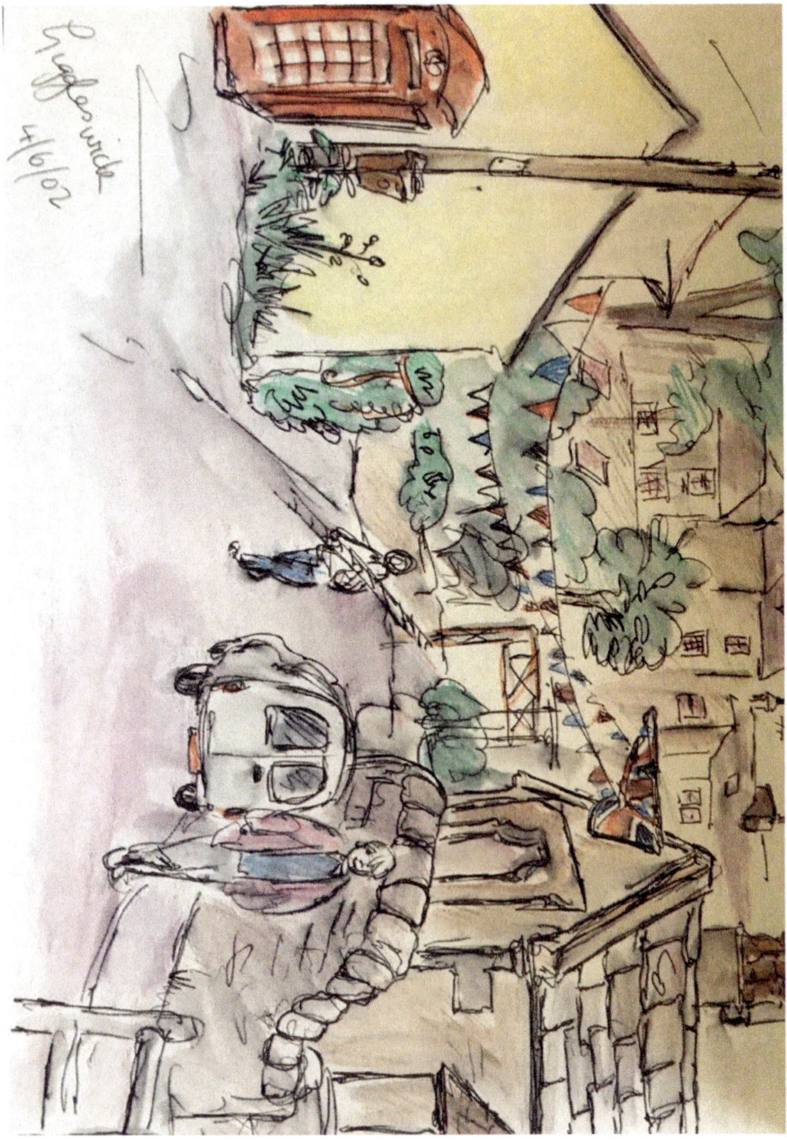
4/6/02

Settle 10/4/99   AMT

Paper Mill, Settle
A. Twisleton

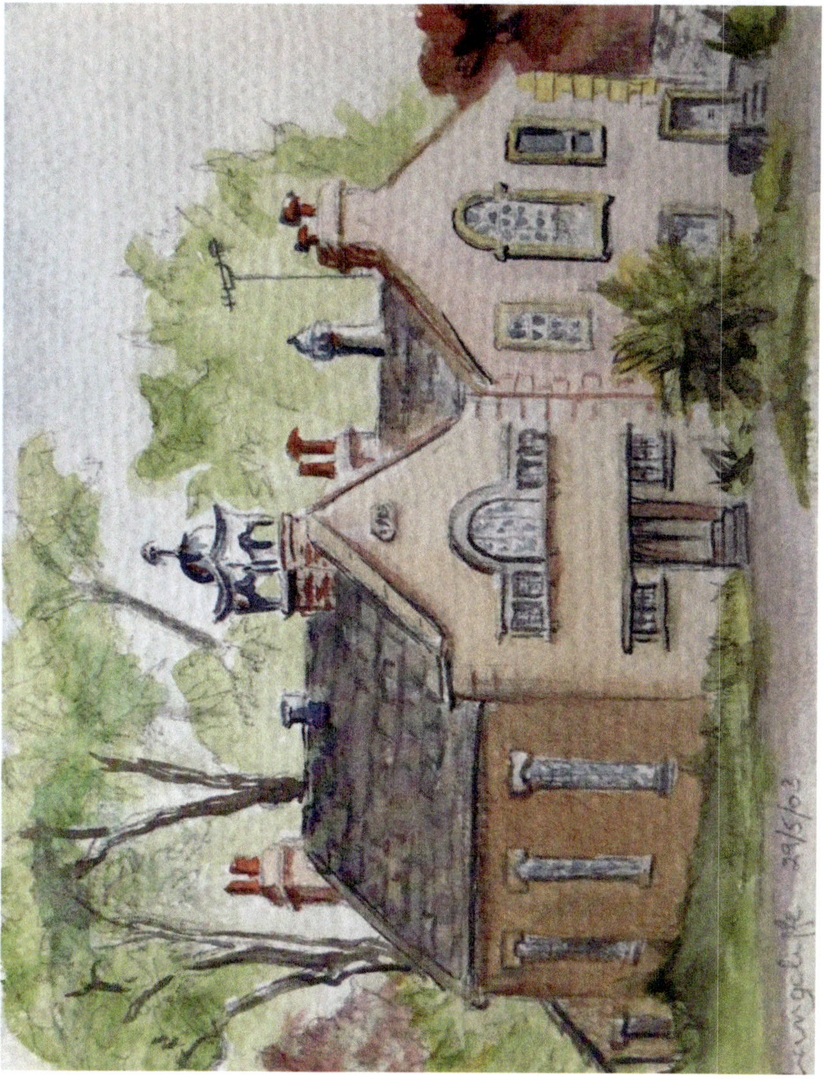
29/5/03

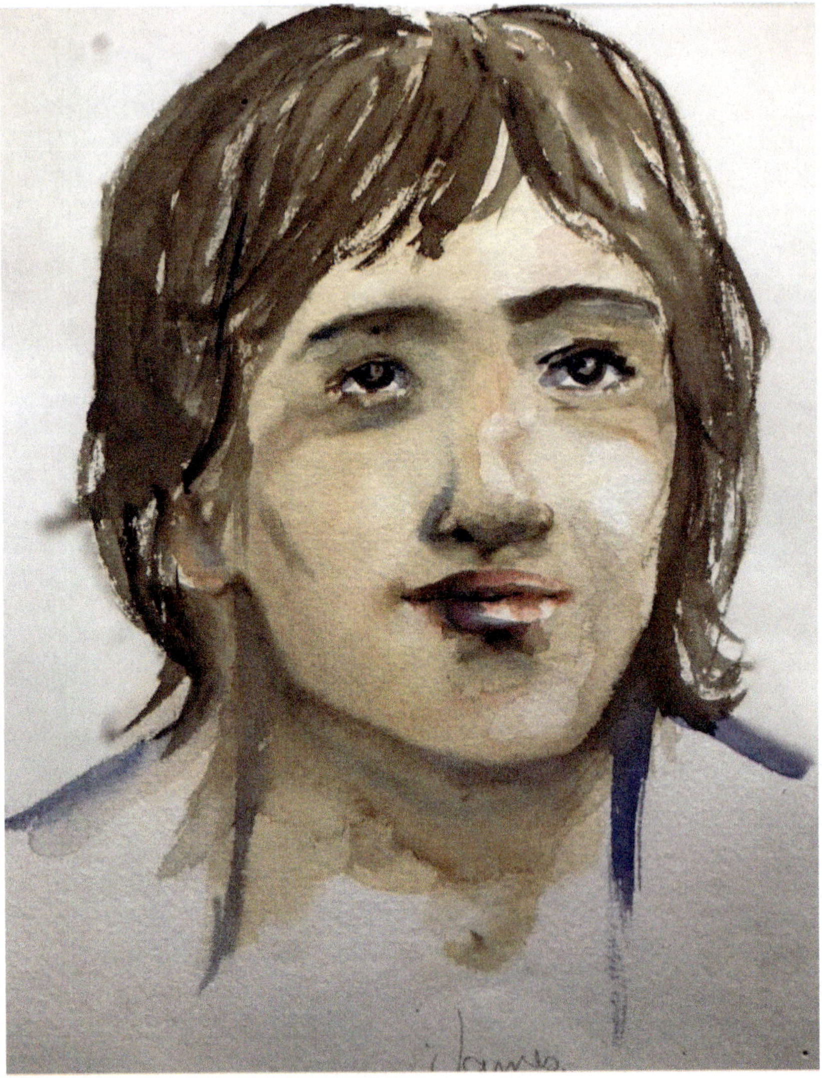

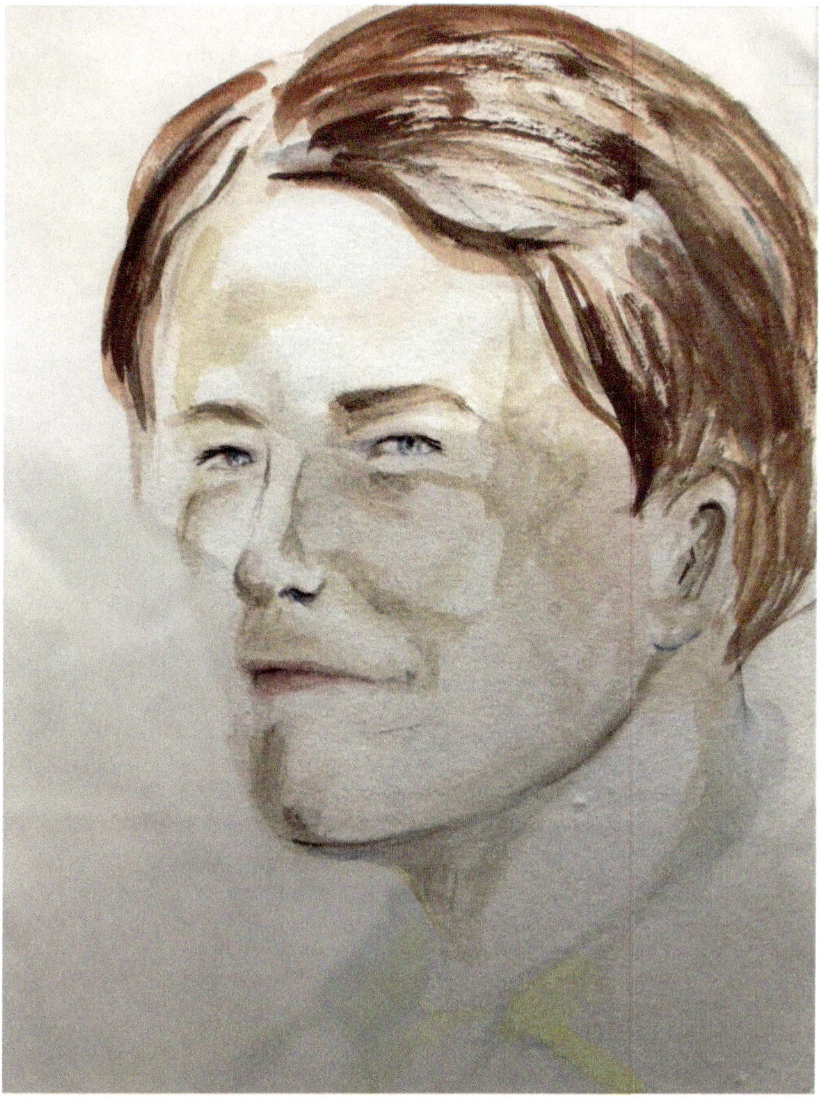

Reading 'Harry Potter'
28th July '00

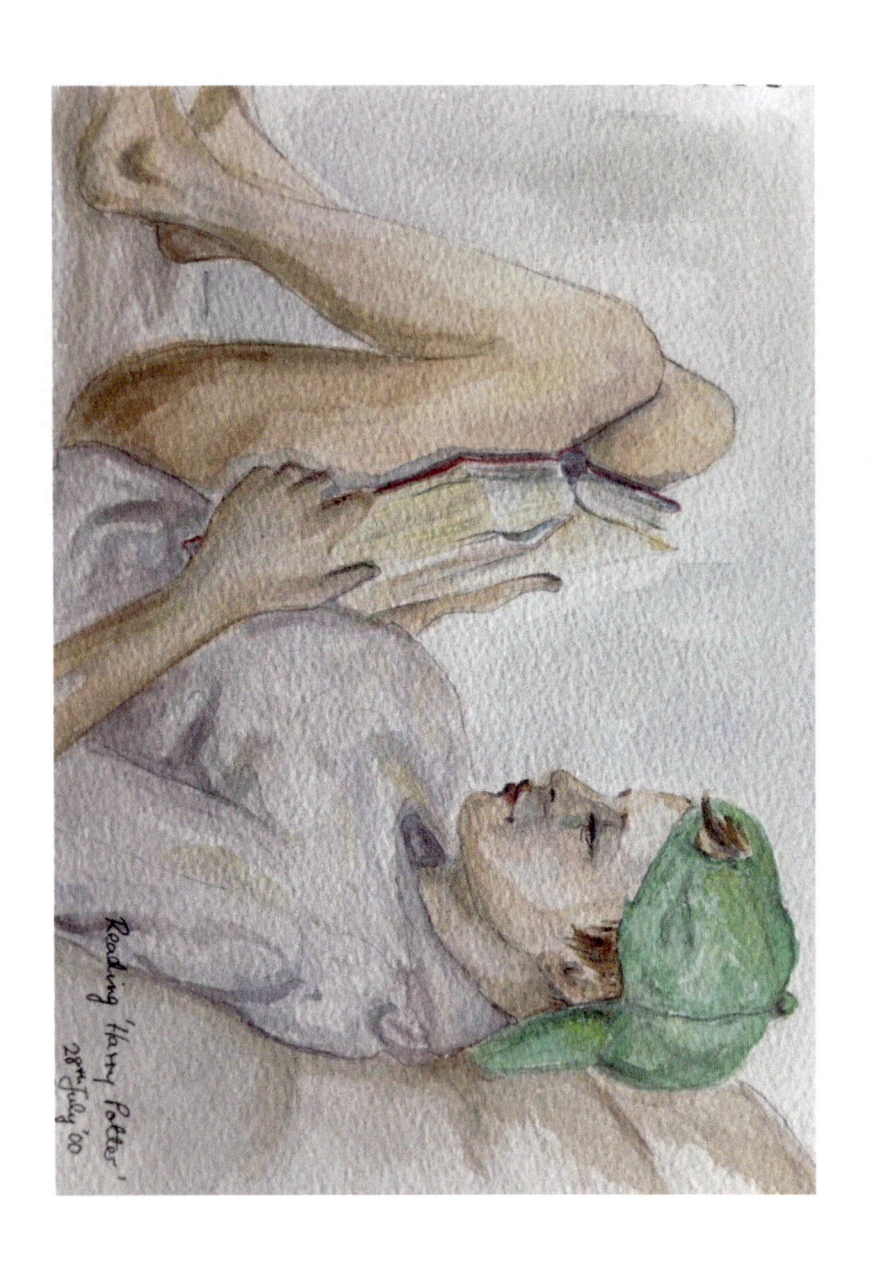

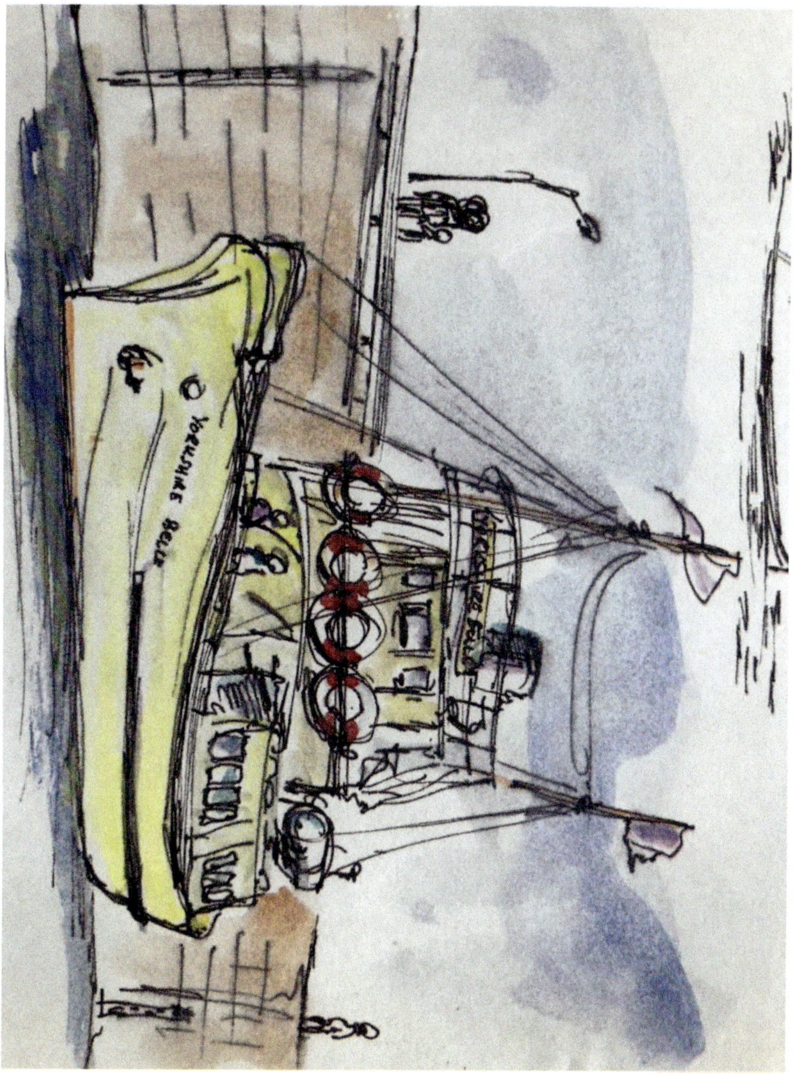
YORKSHIRE BELLE
YORKSHIRE BELLE

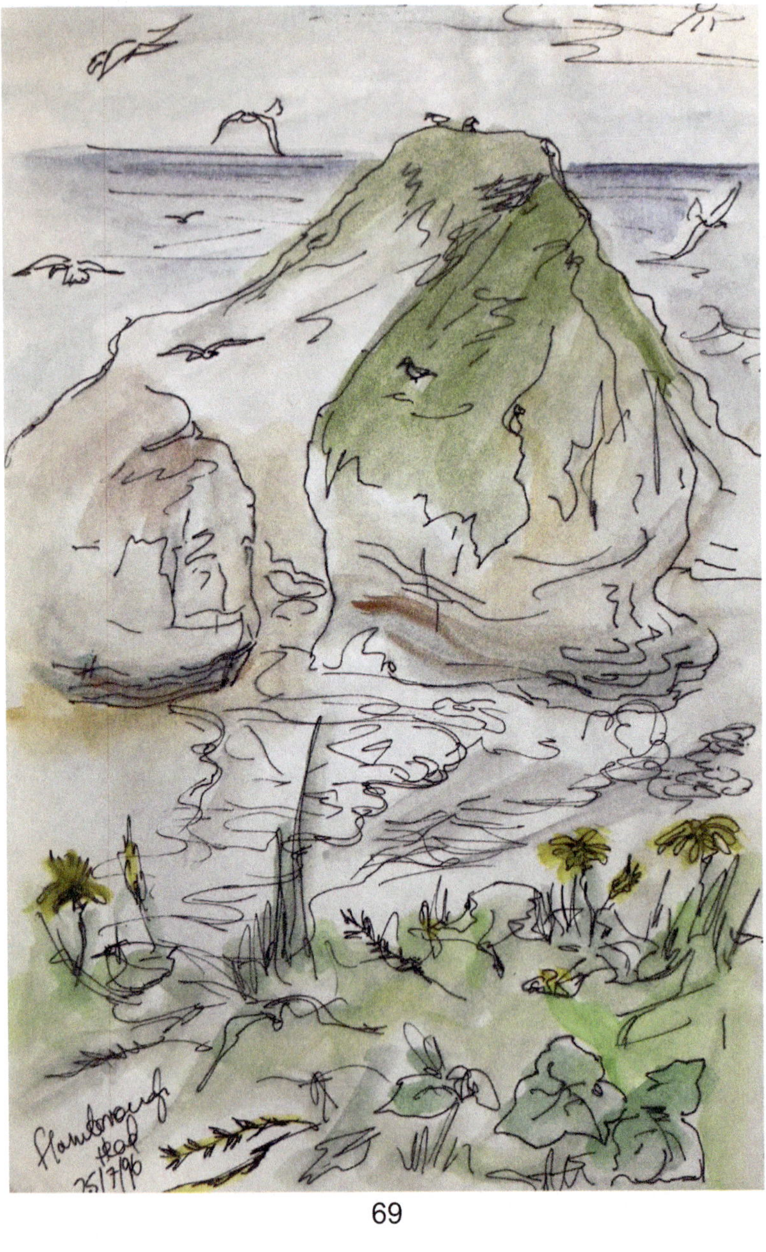
Flamborough Head
25/7/96

Diane McTurk's pet giant otters

Washing Clothes — 31/10/00
the Sandbank
& playing

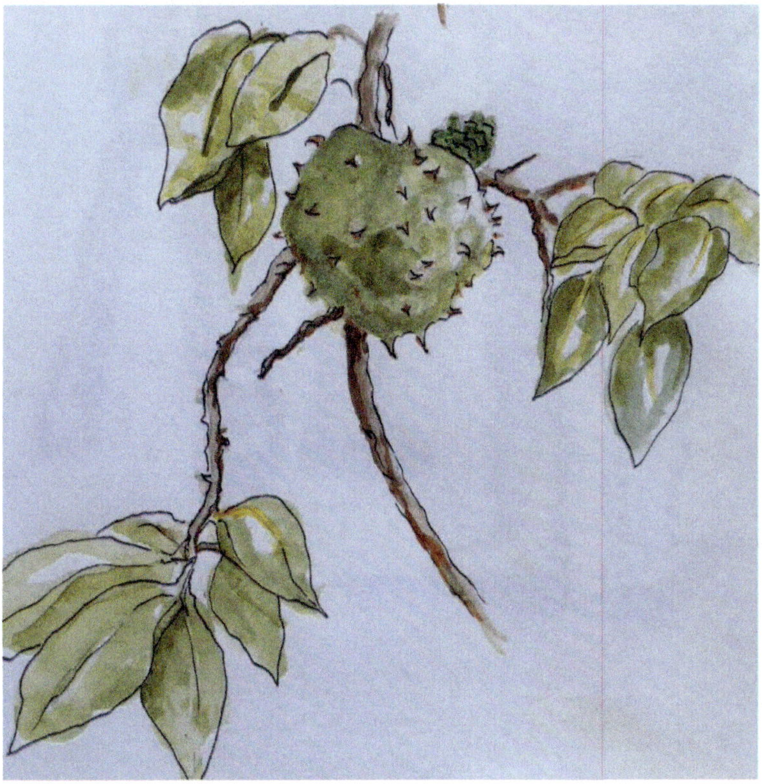

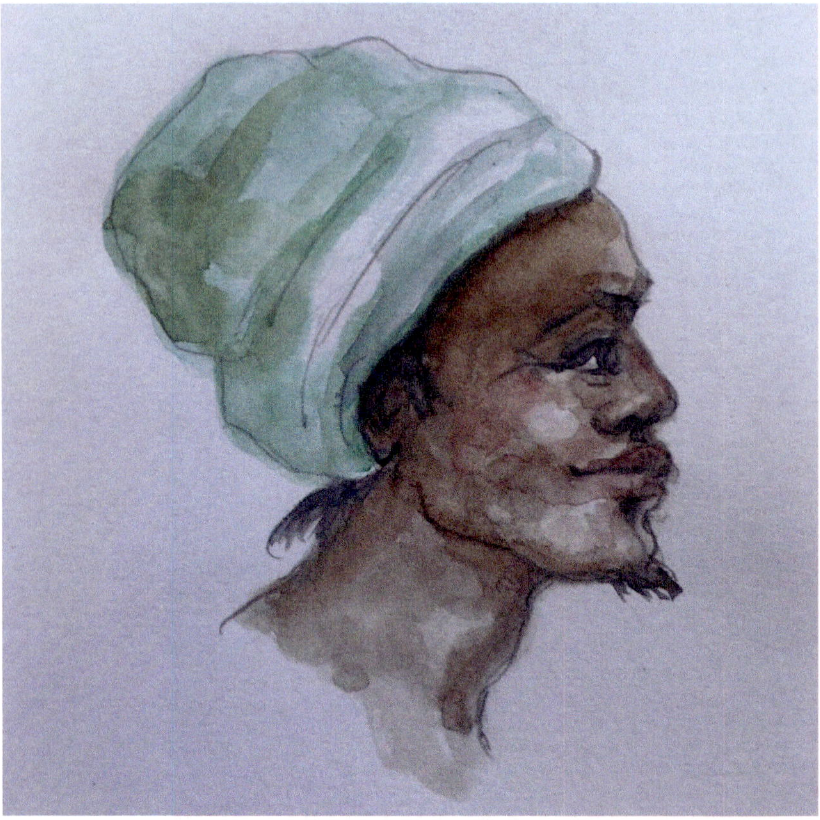

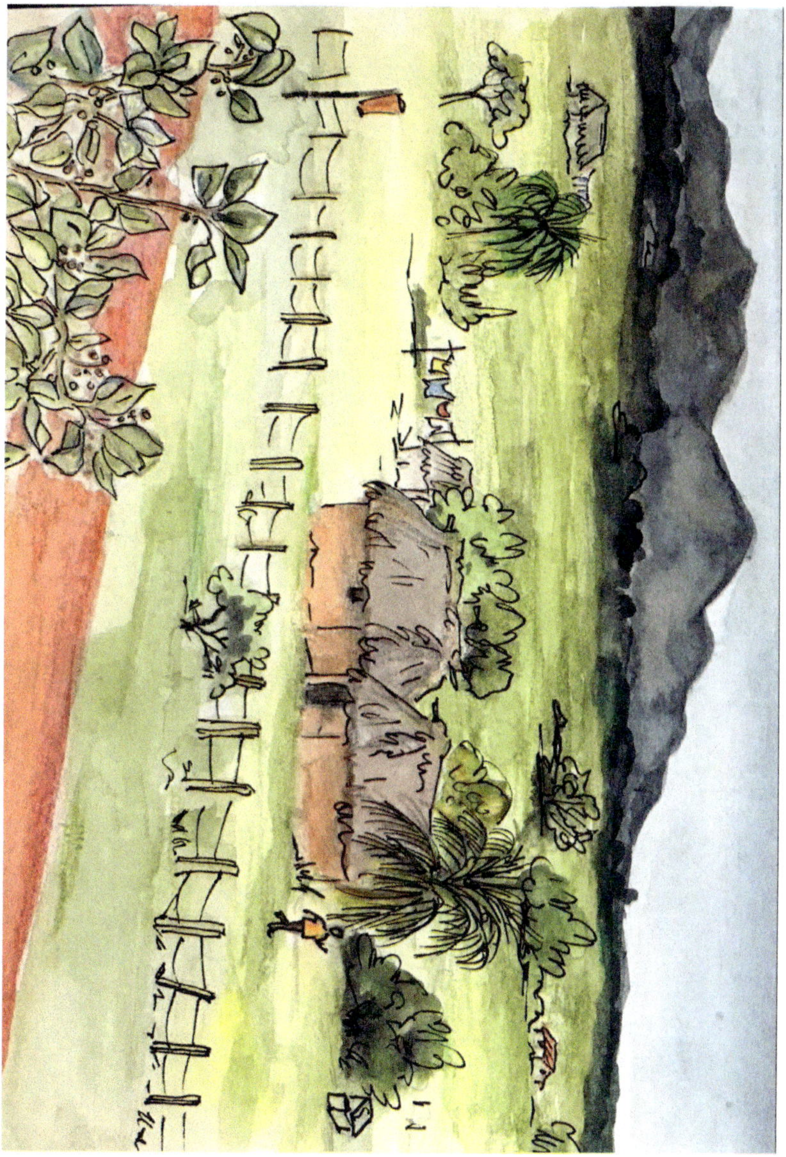

Armadillo killed by Landrover 29/10/00

taken to be cured to be eaten by villagers (+ ourselves)

Cashew Tree
in Guyana
A. Twisleton

Oct 2000
St Sidwell's
Georgetown

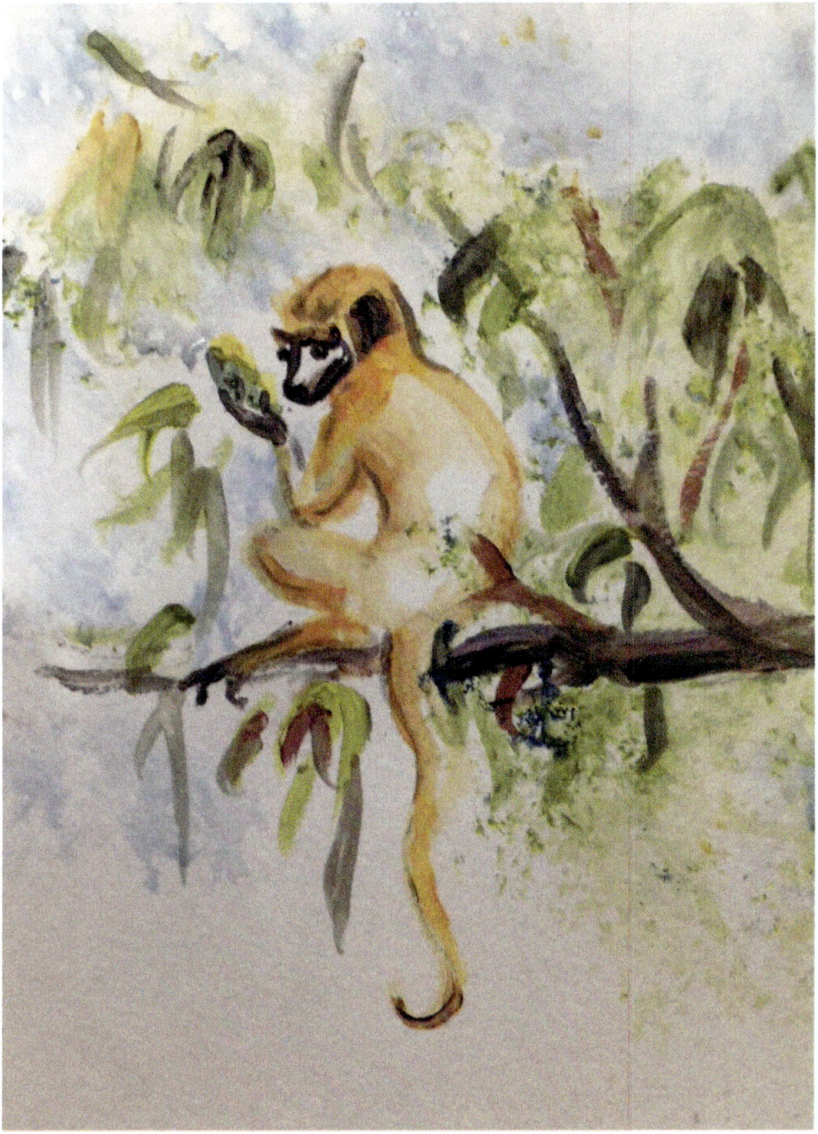

79

Karanambu
Diane McTurk
at the radio

Botanical Gardens
Georgetown

A cool drink in Georgetown (JFT Ag ANT)

John Fernando's Warehouse Ereraflour Ereygana

Great Kiskadee

Manatee

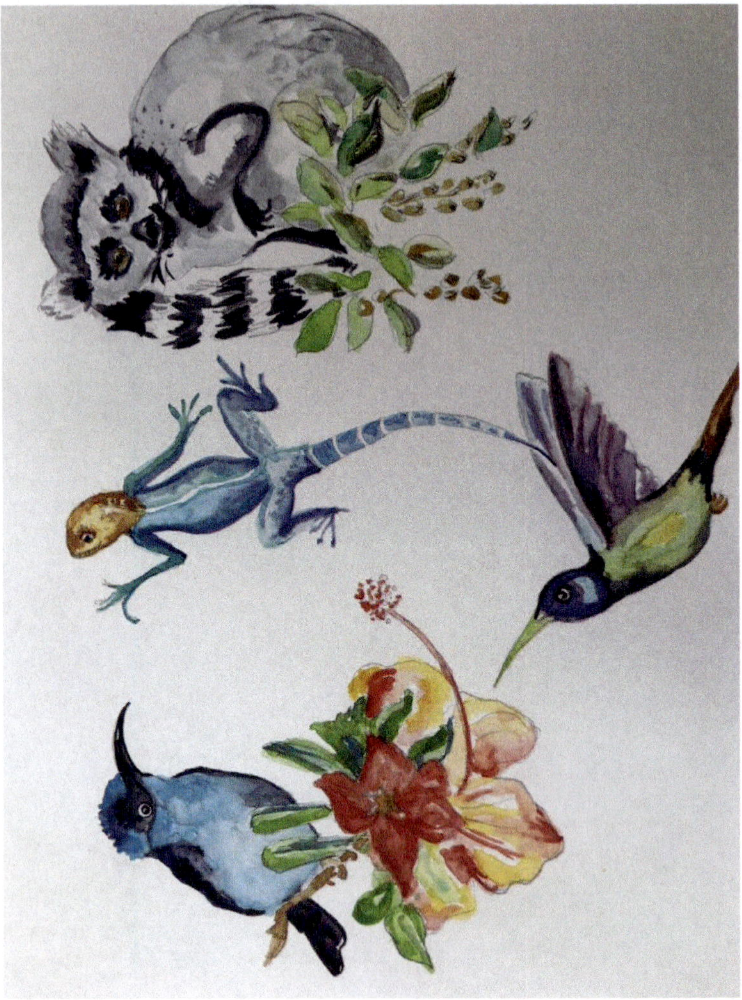

Coventry

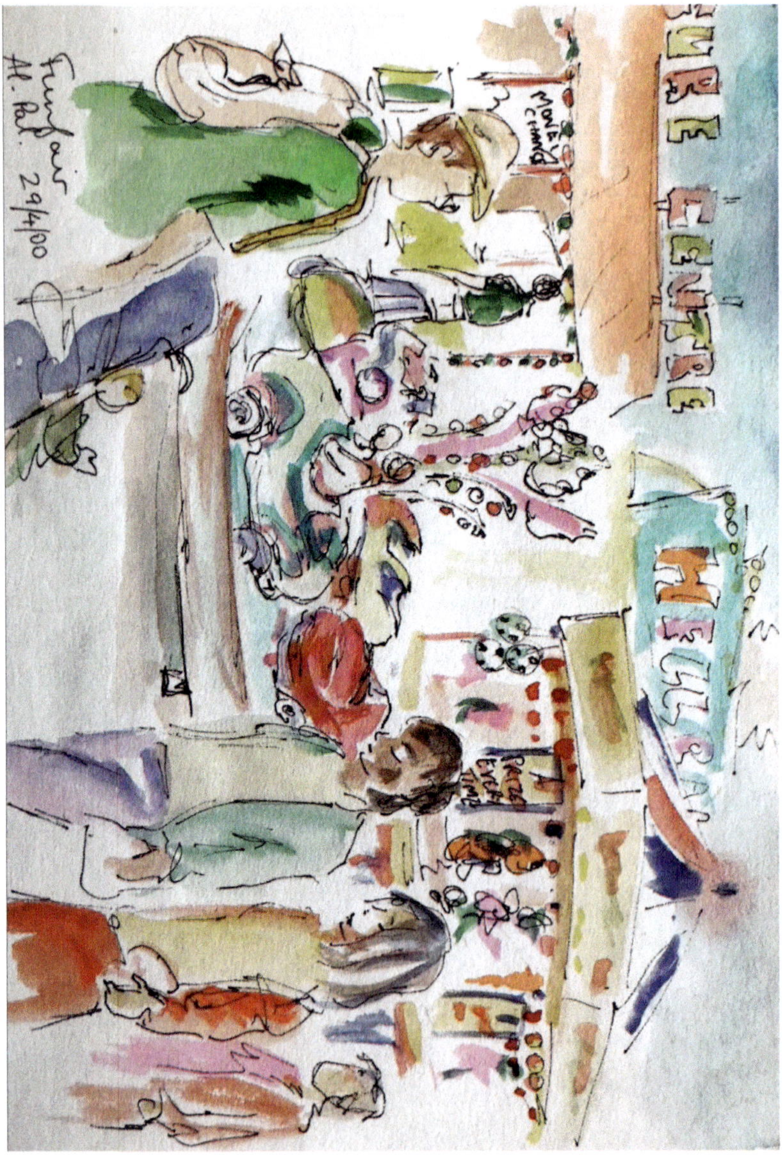
Funfair
Al. Pal. 29/4/00
MONEY CHANGE
PRIZES EVERY TIME

Phoenix Bar, Alexandra Palace 29/4/00

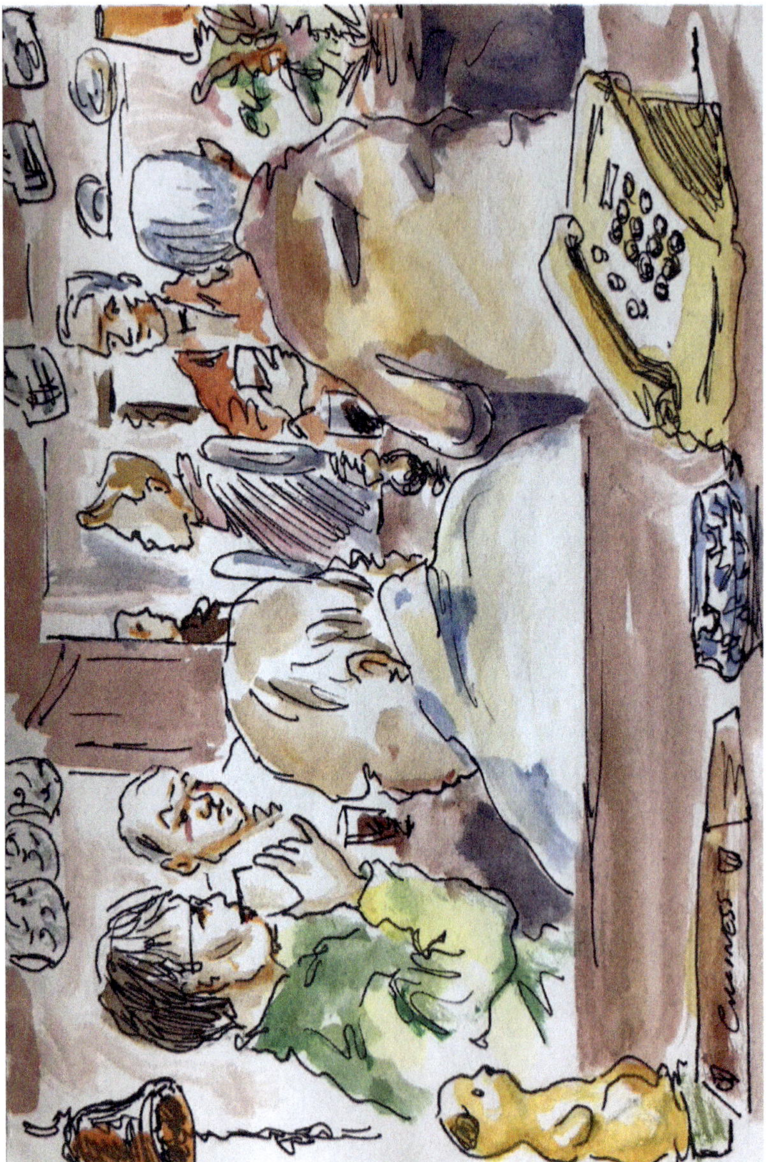
Guinness

Millennium Dome
12/6/00

2002 DISNEY
Paris

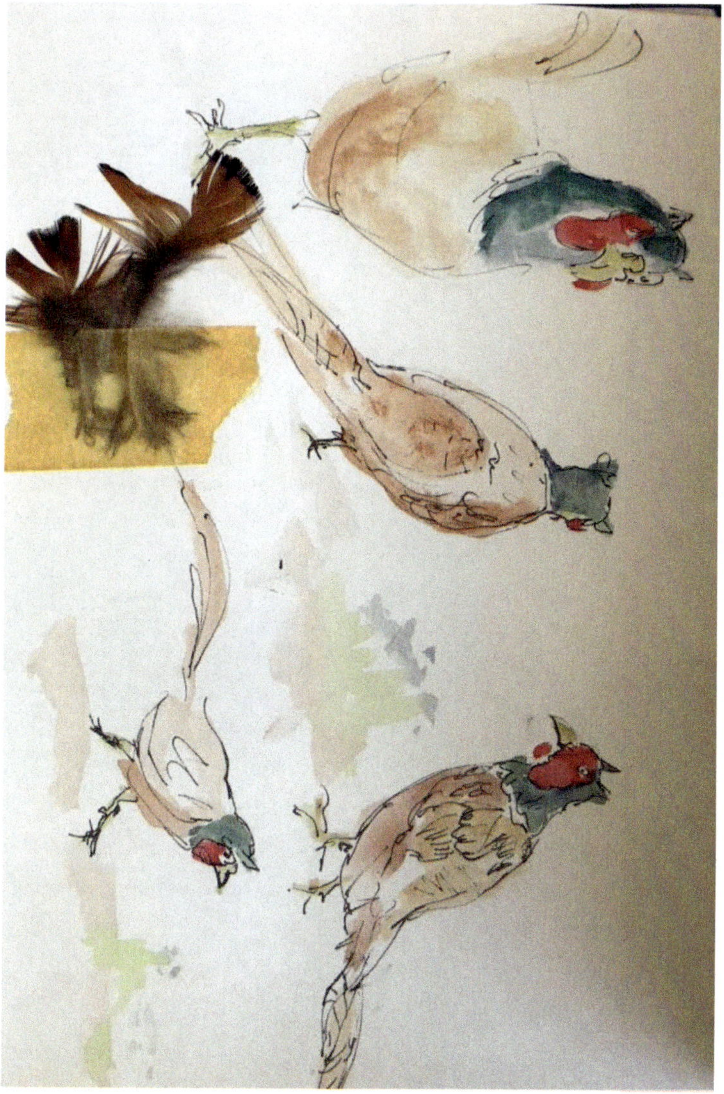

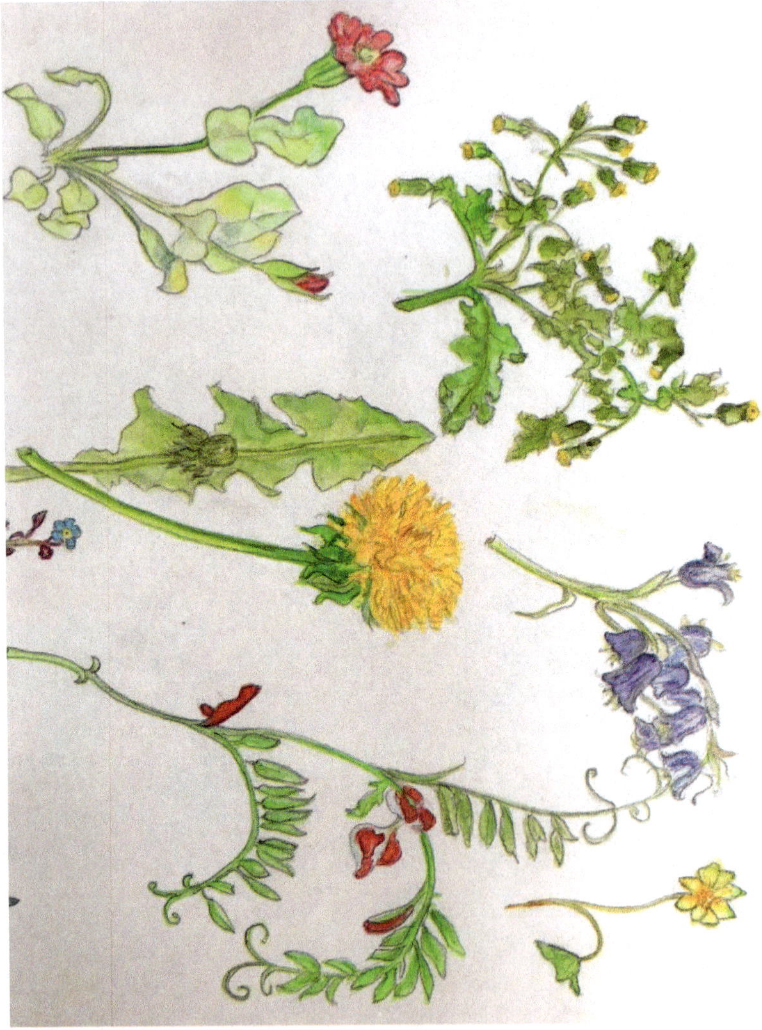

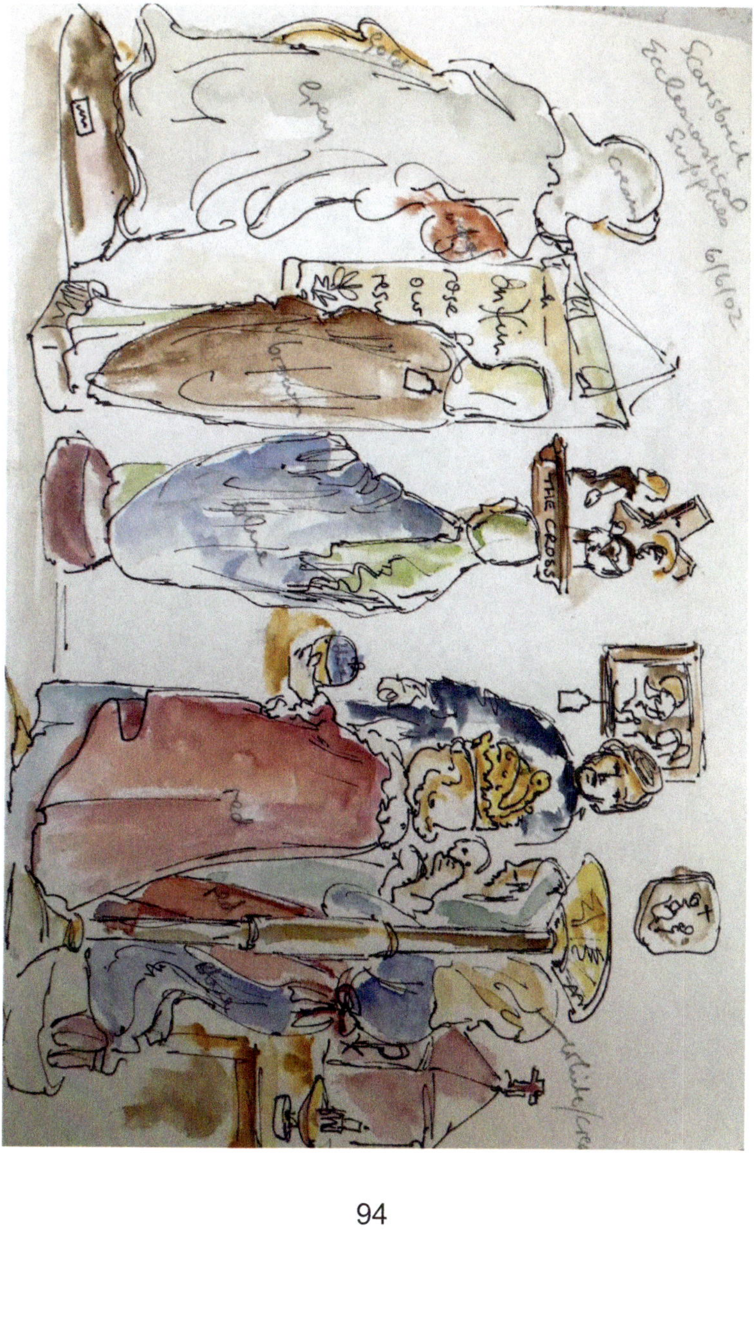
Scarsbrick Ecclesiastical Supplies 6/6/02
THE CROSS
red

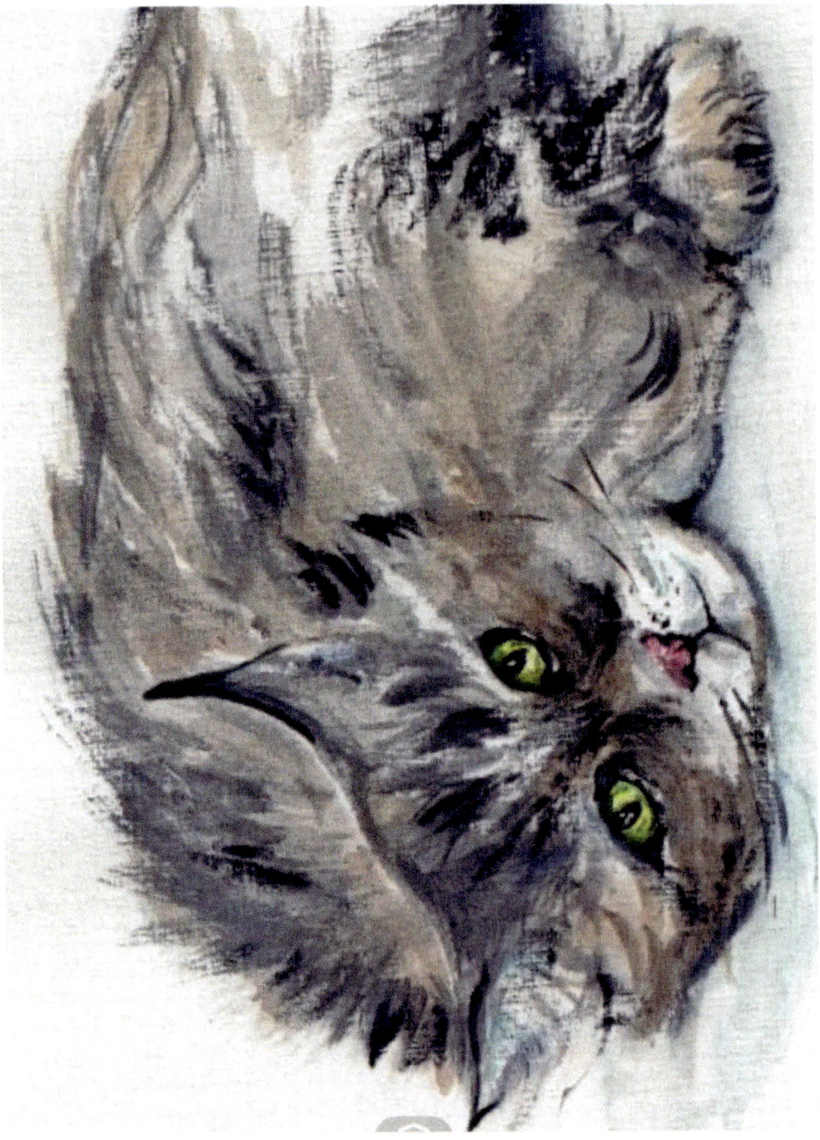

THE VRH TASK

To enable the child to experience *success!*

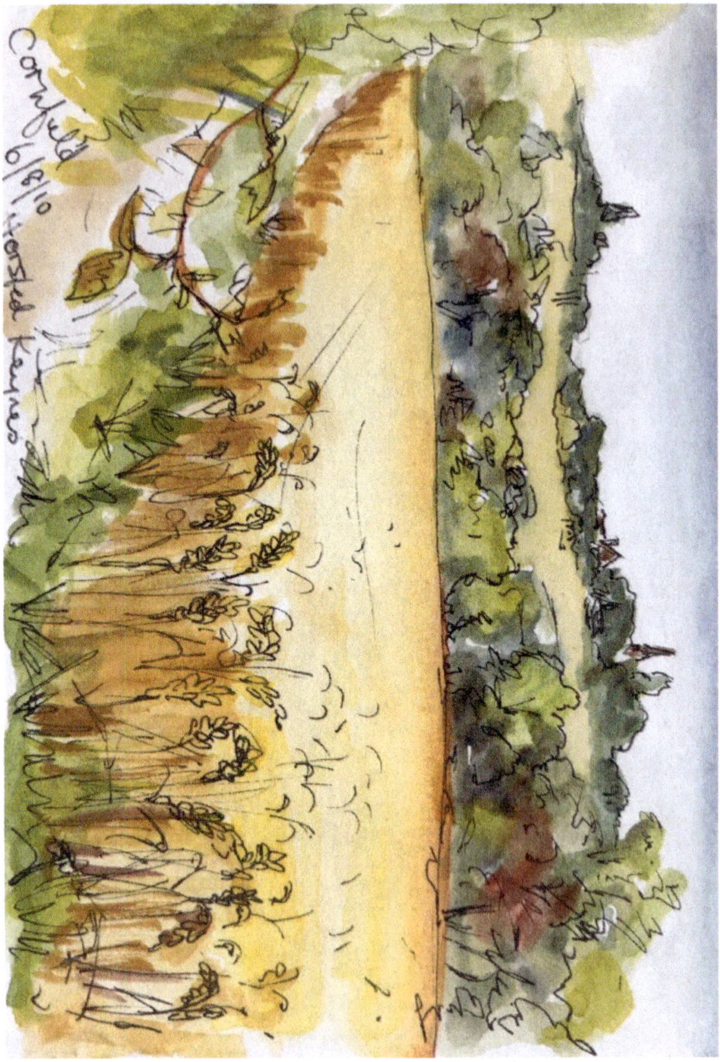
Cornfield 6/8/10 Horsted Keynes

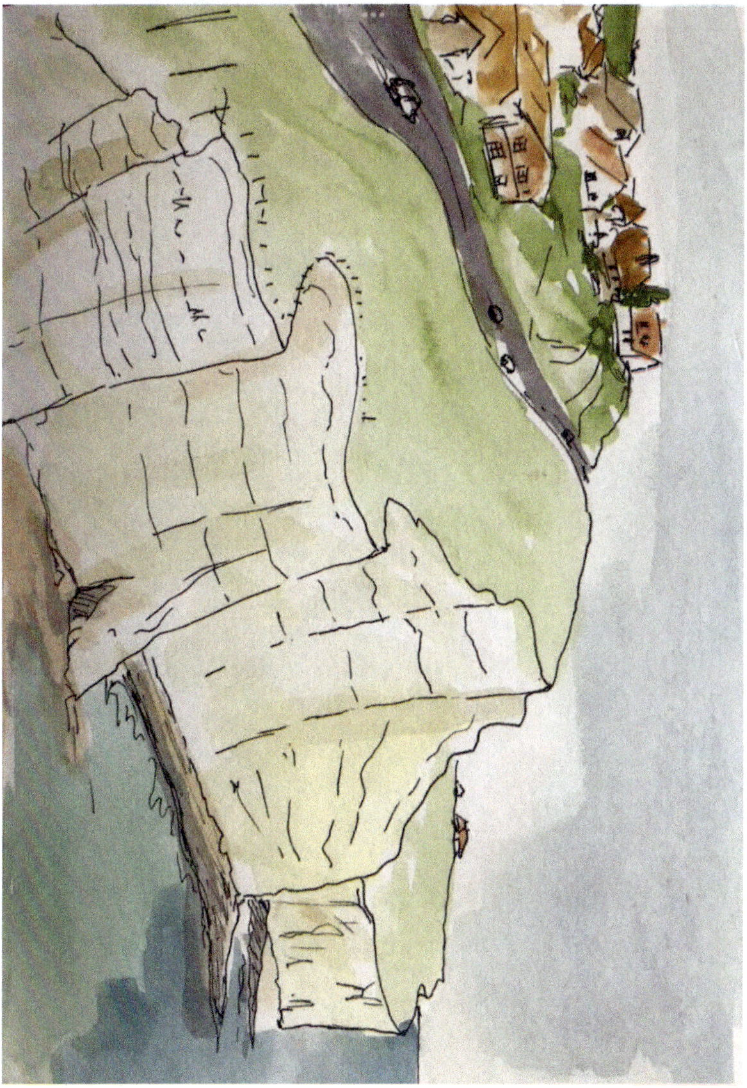

Re-enactment
of Coronation
1st June 2012
St Giles' Church
Horsted Keynes

2015 Family Support Work
Book Sale

Open Garden for Family Support Work

2015

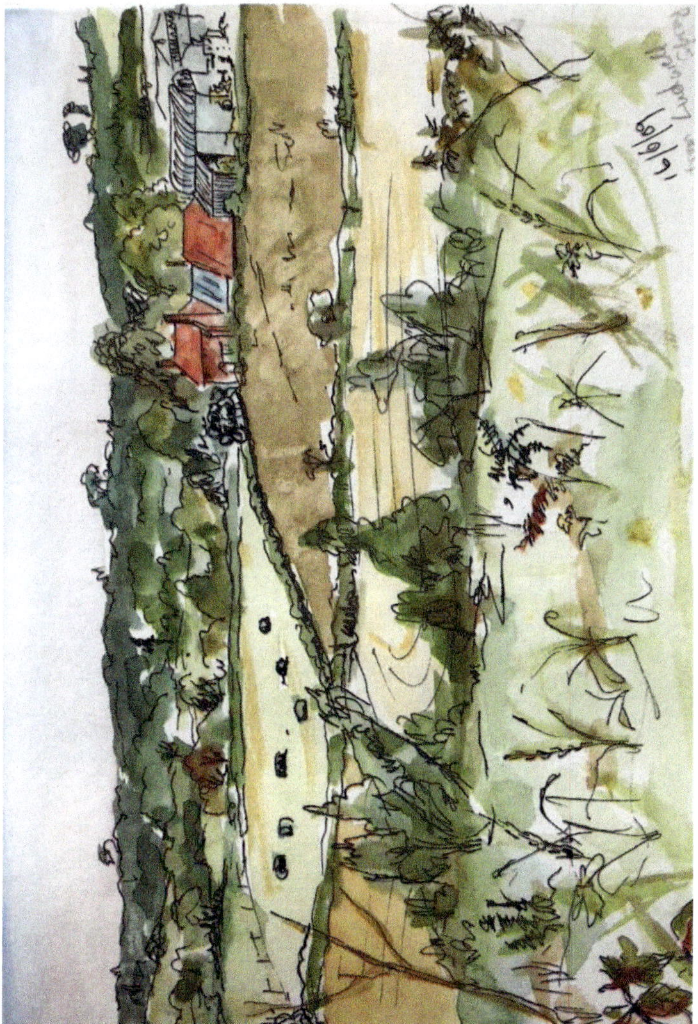

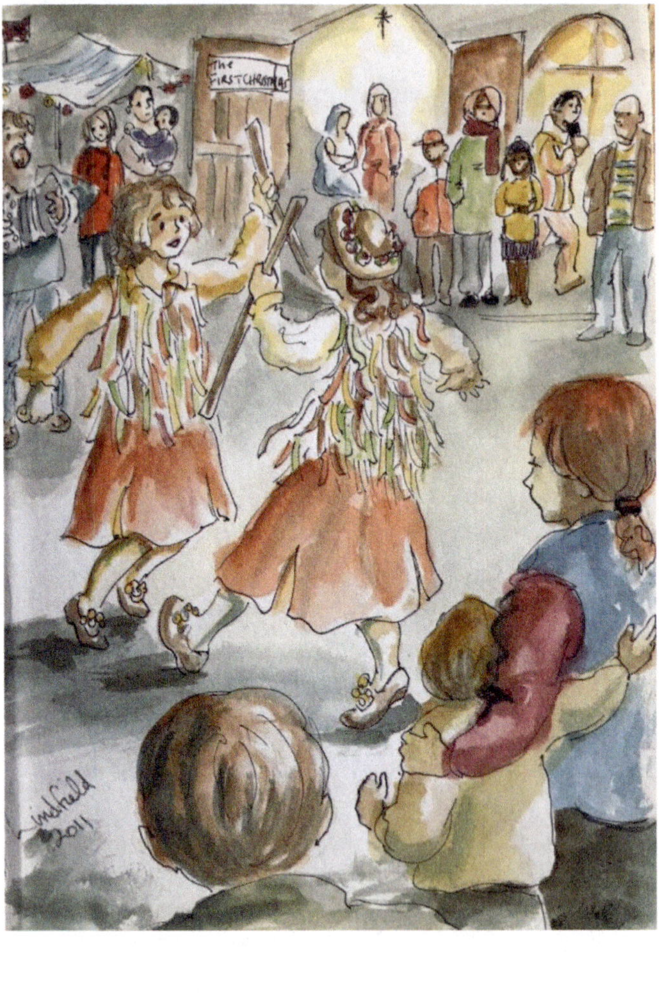
The FIRST CHRISTMAS

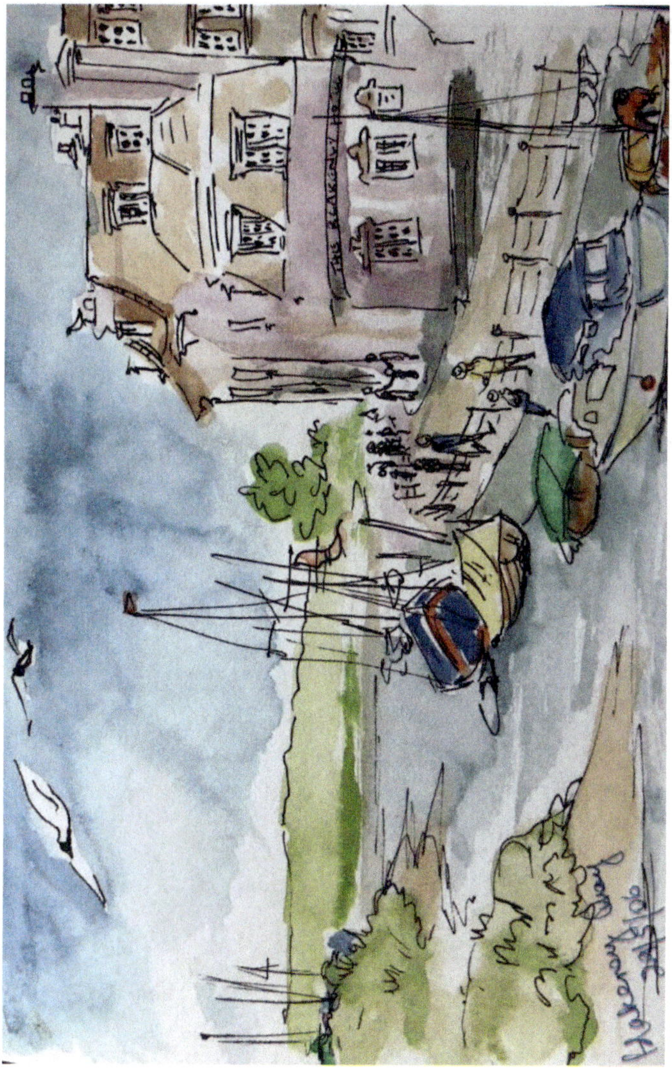

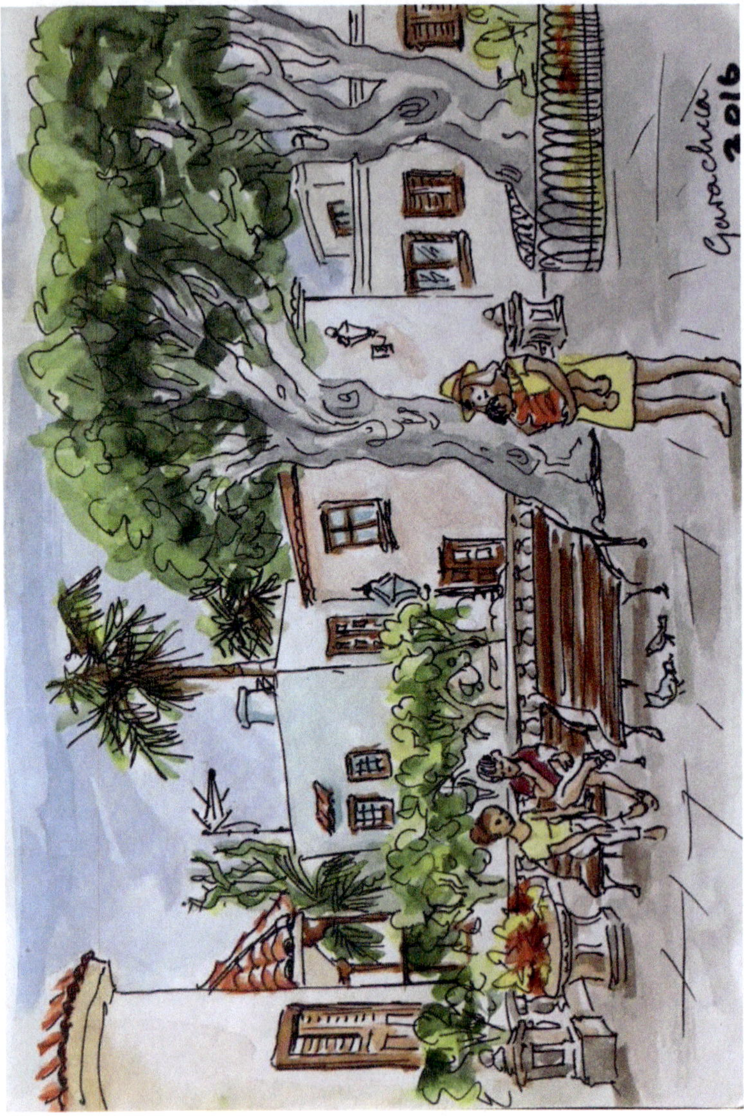
Garachico
2016

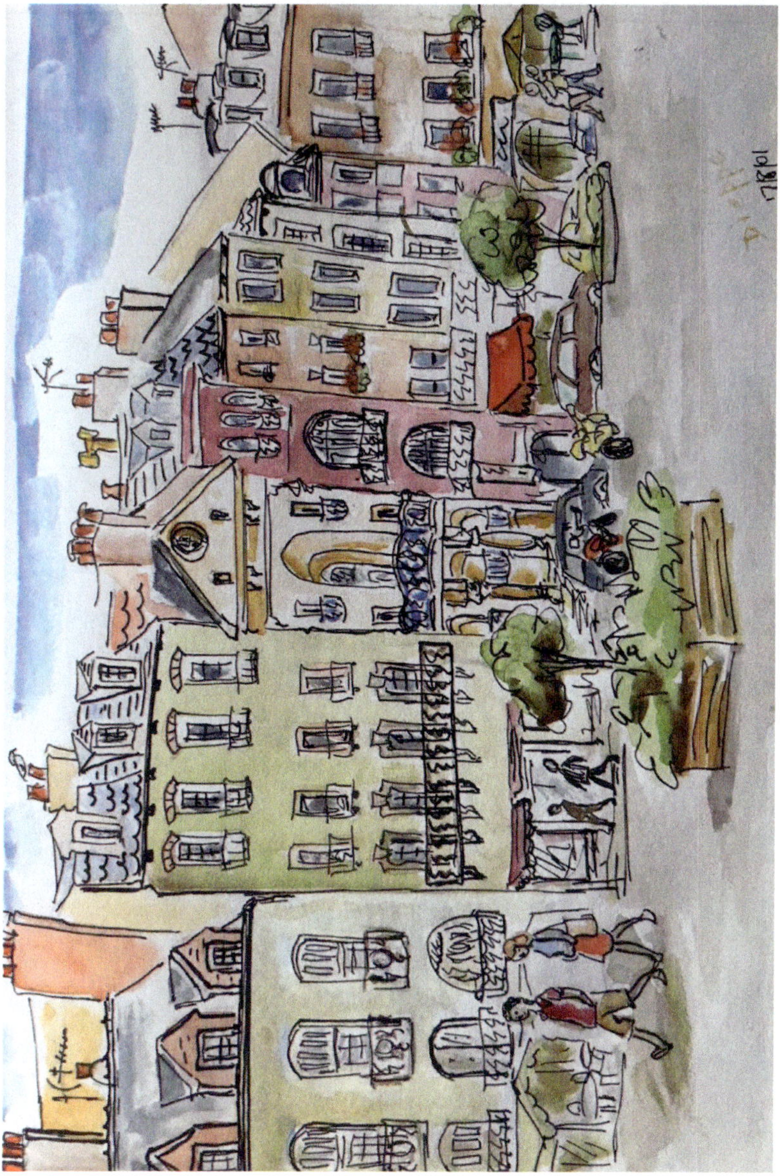

Dunas
Maspalomas 3/2/13

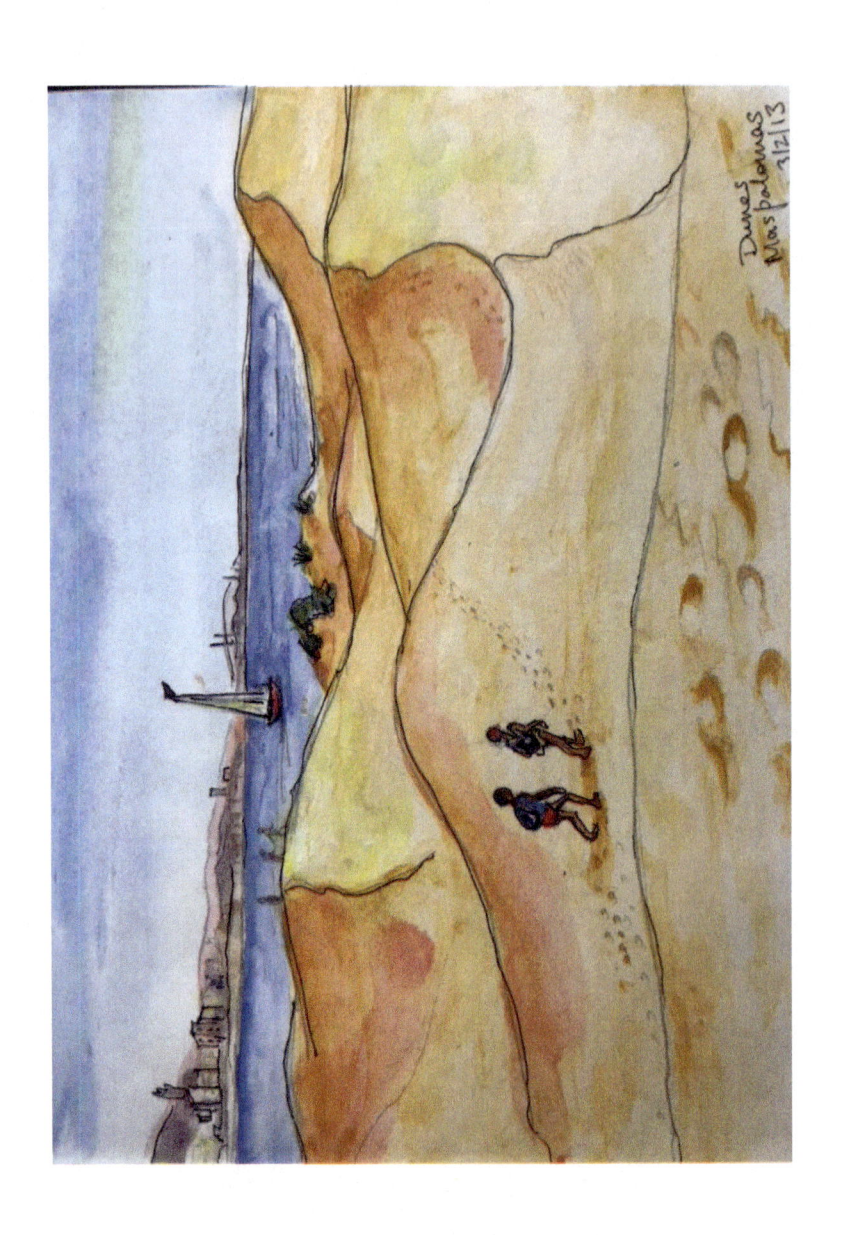

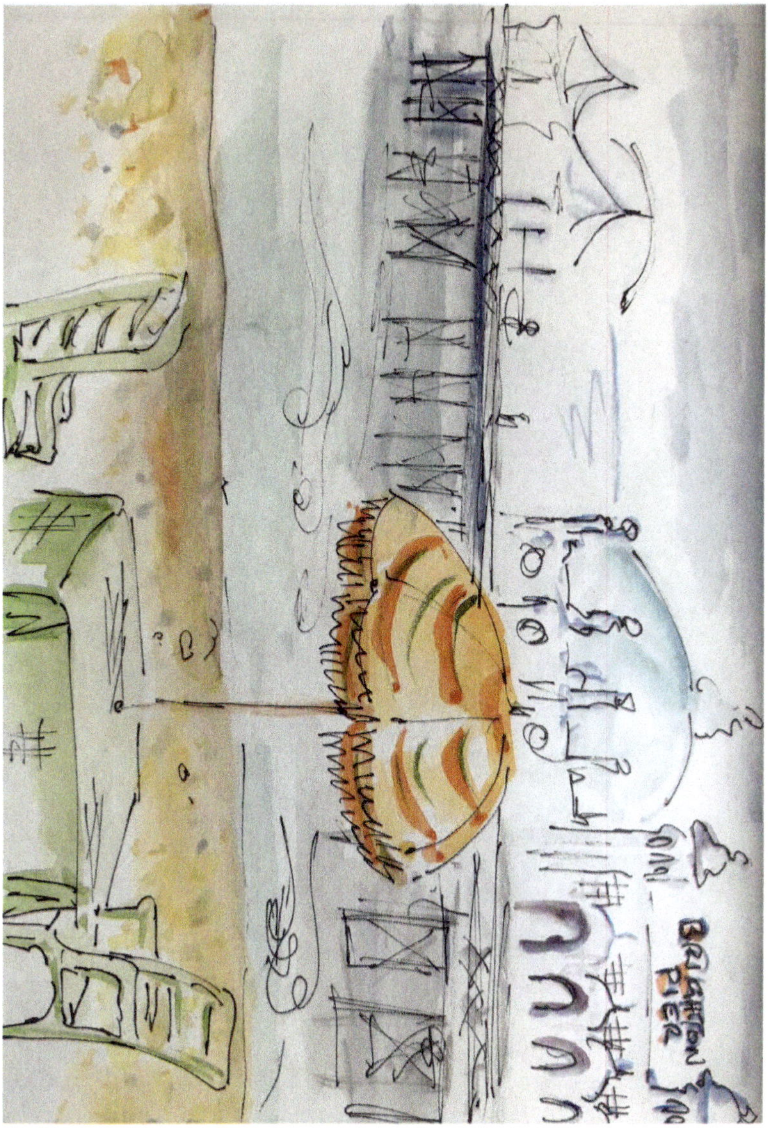
BRIGHTON PIER

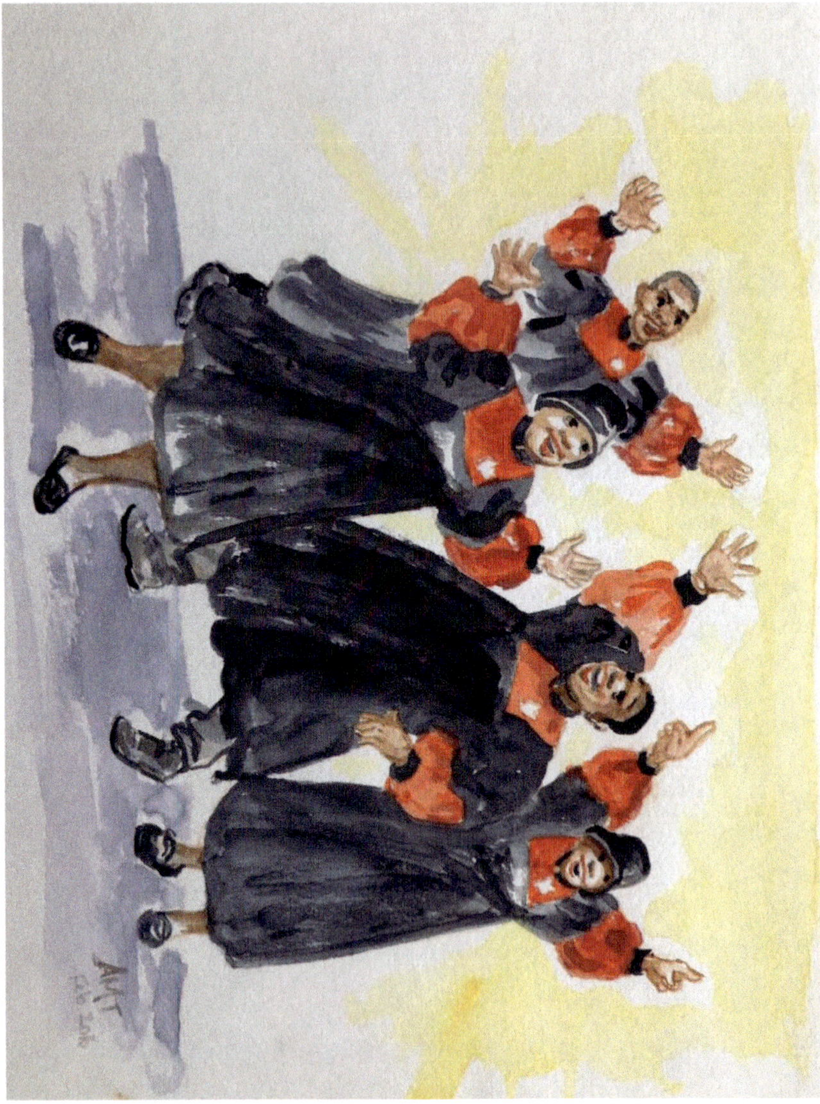

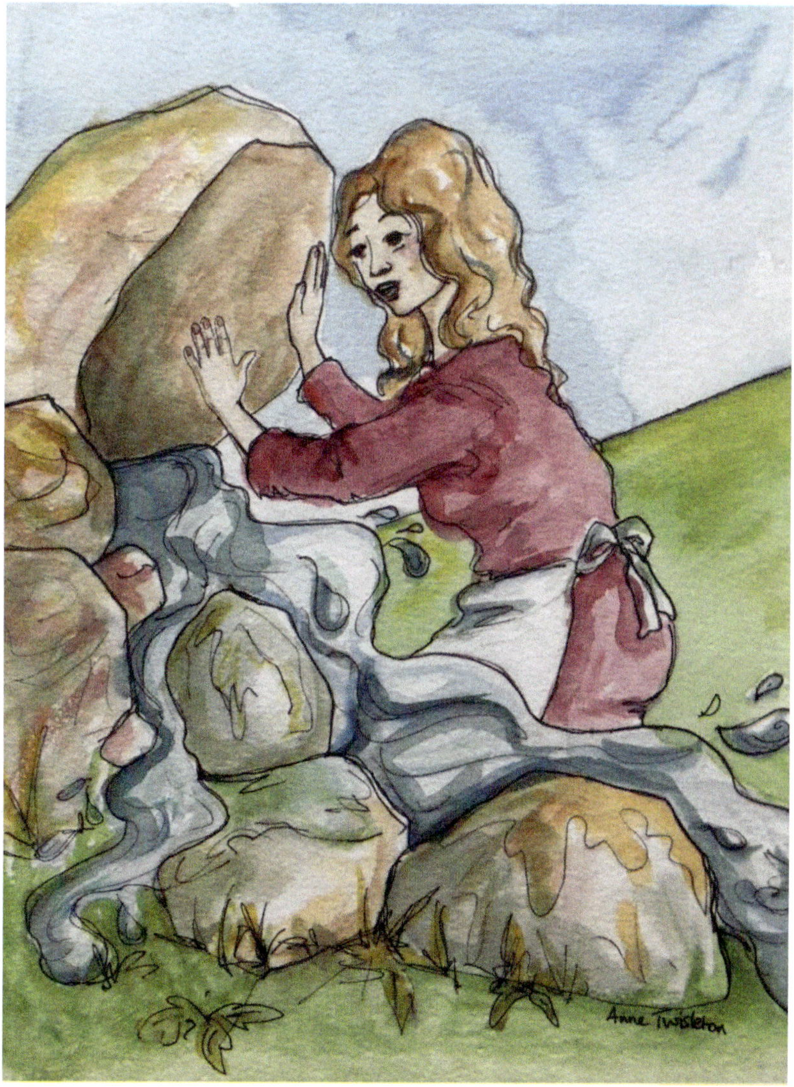
Anne Twisleton

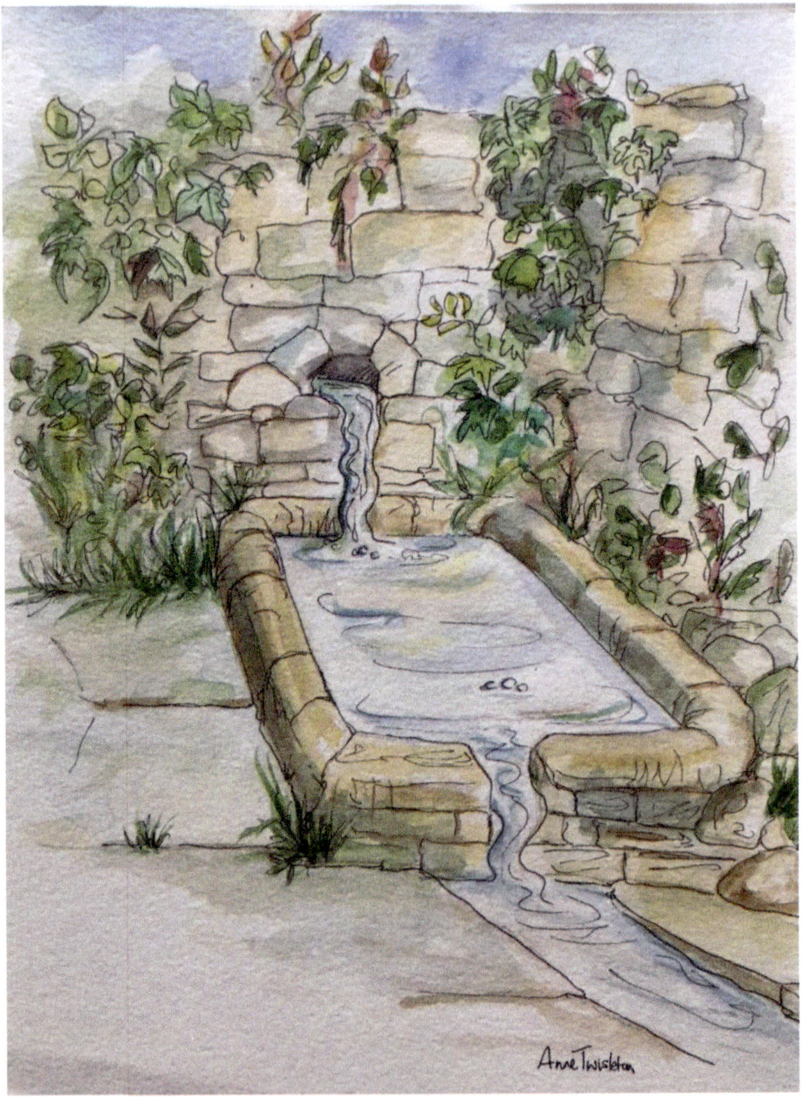
Anne Twisleton

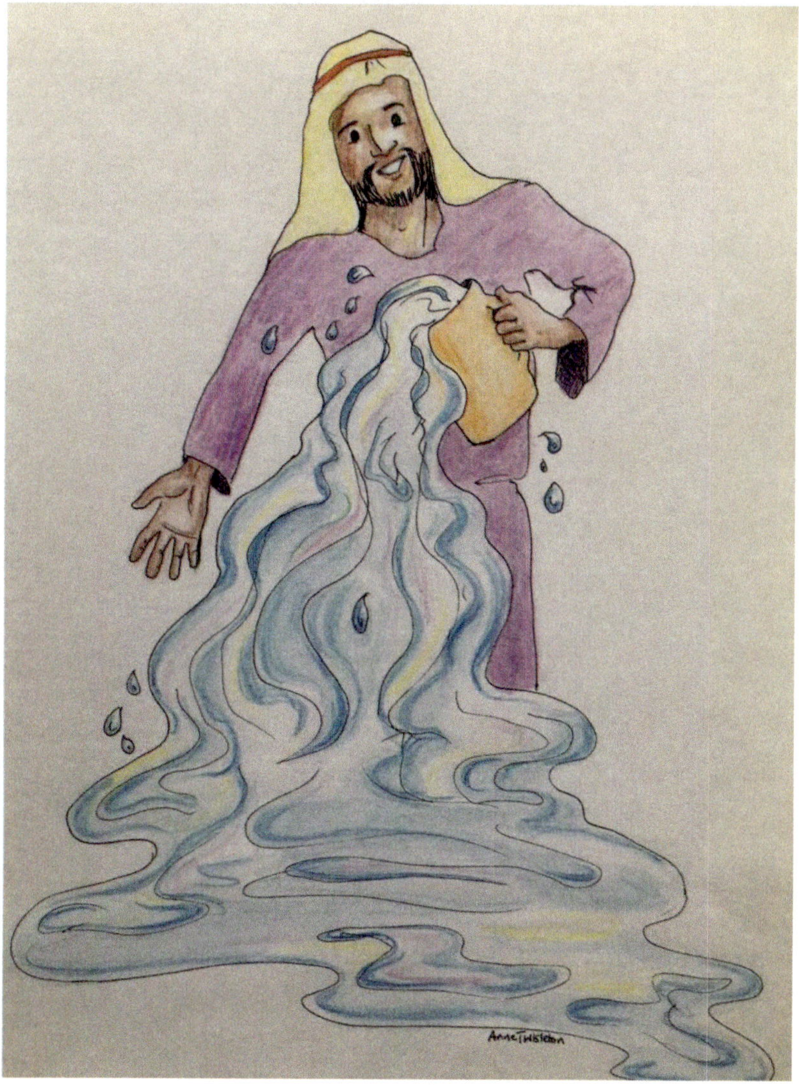

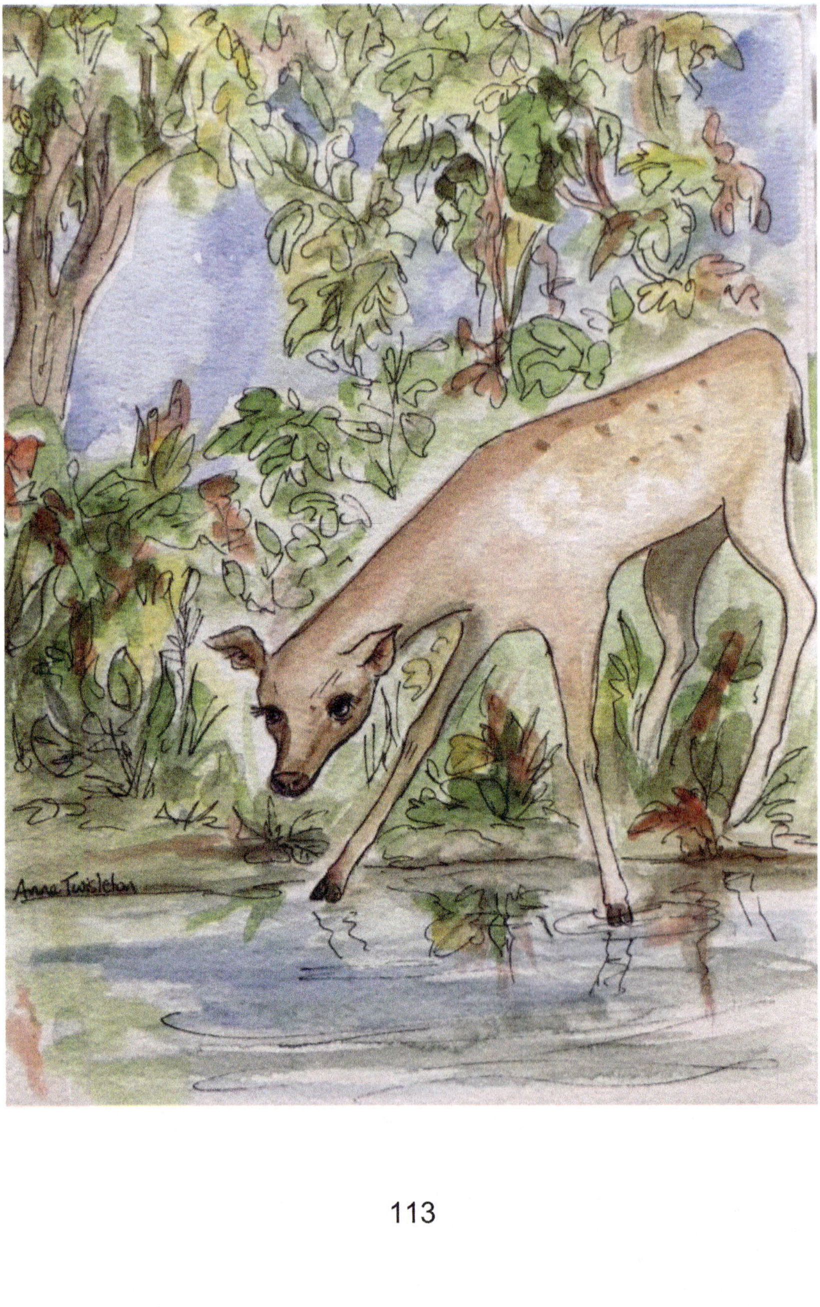
Anna Twisleton

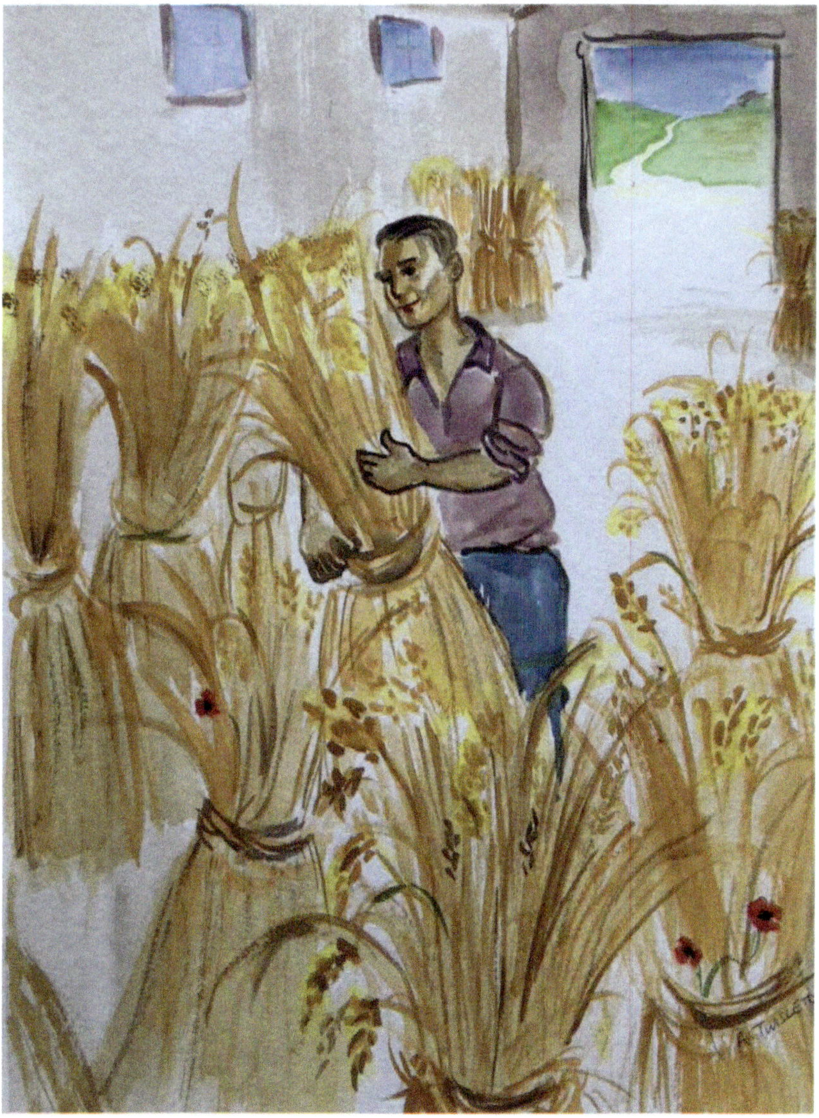

Room
847 Mercure
Paris viens

8   Sussex-by-the-sea

We moved to 27 Gatesmead, Haywards Heath in February 2001 coincident with the national outbreak of foot-and-mouth disease. Public rights of way across land were closed so it was August before we were able to explore the Sussex countryside. In the wake of previous walking in London John published 'Forty Walks from Ally Pally', a best-seller and postscript to our time in London. In Sussex we had more green space to expand into even if that expansion was delayed six months by foot and mouth. Moving was a wrench, especially heading further from our parents in Yorkshire. Anne's dad Ervin died aged 82 in 2000 before our move and we were able to be at his bedside and support his widow, Doris. In 2002 we celebrated John's mother Elsie's 80th birthday in the Grand Hotel, Brighton, Anne's 50th at The Ritz, John's 25th anniversary of priesting at St Richard, Haywards Heath and the marriage of David and Denise at St George, Enfield, London celebrated by Fr John. Leaving London meant no work discontinuity for Anne as I continued working for the Sussex branch of Volunteer Reading Help but after a year, sadly, it closed. With John, though rooted at St Richard's, moving between Churches on Sundays the family chose to worship at a Church of evangelical tradition close to our home: All Saints, Lindfield. I applied successfully to be its Administrator, one of a staff of seven serving a church of several hundred members with dozens of organisations springing from it. It was a busy office, great fun, with no two days alike. I was five minutes by car from work in the beautiful village of Lindfield, with its medieval church and houses, a duck pond and walks in open countryside a 2 minute stroll from the church. Haringey seemed far away and long ago! James was a proper computer geek, putting his mum and dad straight in a way worthy of brother David working then and now in the IT Department of University College, London. At that time our son John regularly visited Gothenburg, Sweden linked to romantic involvement then with Theresa whom he met on pilgrimage to Walsingham. John worked as a roofer with Theresa's dad but, though the two remain friends, he returned to live with us initially, moving on to live nearby in Burgess Hill qualifying in kitchen work. From leaving London in 2001 Fr John and I have lived happily in Sussex-by-the-sea in three locations around Haywards Heath, with easy visits to the south coast, London and, on occasion, abroad to the Caribbean via Gatwick.

As Mission & Renewal Advisor in Chichester Diocese my work covered over 500 churches compared to the 100 in Edmonton Area. I was now a team leader with paid and volunteer officers serving church growth, evangelism, interfaith liaison, liturgy, music, spirituality and stewardship. Chichester Diocese covers East and West Sussex and the city of Brighton & Hove stretching 100 miles along the south coast so my base in Haywards Heath was strategic minimising distance travelled to advise parishes from Rye west to Chichester and Crawley south to Brighton. In 2004 I headed up an ecumenical year of prayer across Sussex served by an audio CD 'Entering the prayer of Jesus' broadcast on Premier Radio. In 2007 helped by my friend, now Judge, James Dingemans I conducted a belief survey across Sussex with conclusions broadcast on Premier coincident with a series 'Firmly I Believe' on the creed, sacraments, commandments and prayer. Other series looked at 'Frequently Asked Questions' about faith and 'Speaking up for

Jesus'. My eight years work as advisor culminated, like that in the Edmonton Area, in a Eucharist 'Caritas 08' which the Bishop celebrated 2008 in Brighton Centre. Parishes prepared for this by setting priorities and bringing Bishop John Hind their mission plans to Brighton. I worked by phone and visiting to engage clergy, encouraging and challenging them and seeking access to their church councils. My experience was that roughly a third of churches were succeeding, a third failing and a third marking time and it was this last group I tried to engage with the officers of my team. It was a joy to see the difference made to churches by setting priorities and to individuals by seeking spiritual direction and costlier discipleship. After Caritas 08 Bishop Hind offered me the parish of St Giles, Horsted Keynes where demands of caring for 2,000 people could be balanced with keeping up writing and broadcasting.

As we got the last boxes unpacked in Horsted Keynes Rectory, I began to work as a Pampered Chef consultant, demonstrating recipes and good quality kitchen equipment in people's homes, which was very enjoyable. Then in September 2009 I was asked to work 3 days a week for the Diocesan Family Support Work, which offers help to families in crisis all over Sussex. It worked well with Pampered Chef, which I could do a couple of evenings a month. I also used to look forward to Saturday mornings, when I would usually go to Burgess Hill with a team from various churches who offer "Healing on the Streets", praying for those who would like prayer, and seeing great blessings ensue. Friends from all over were drawn to visit us taking in the Bluebell railway, former Prime Minister Harold Macmillan's grave and the gem of a Sussex Church that's stood proud for 1000 years. Both James and John worked initially nearby in residential homes and we exchanged regular visits with Dave, Denise and our grandchildren Victoria (b 2005) and Robyn (b 2010) in London and our mothers Elsie in Settle and Doris in Shipley.

I enjoyed my last parish with the asset of Anne at my side in ministry working in a beautiful village with great people. St Giles was near to 'middle of the road' churchmanship with gifted lay folk who drew with us on both catholic and evangelical riches and insight. There was excellent Christian engagement with a tight knit village community strengthened in my day by a venture led by Churchwarden James Nicholson instituting a monthly village lunch. My transition from diocesan sector went well. I didn't miss the committees, gaining more involvement with people opening up to God through spiritual direction and continuing as an ideas man not least in the pulpit. The bishop and my successor as adviser wanted me to keep on leading for the Diocese on Christian apologetics - not 'apologising' for faith but helping give an 'apologia' or reasoned defence for belief. Bible Reading Fellowship commissioned me as author of Meet Jesus (2011), Using the Jesus Prayer (2014) and Experiencing Christ's Love (2017) (see Appendix 2) and I kept up my involvement broadcasting Thought of the Day on Premier Christian Radio and on their Sunday morning news programme. I became the 'window priest' with my eight year tenure as Rector including the introduction of glass doors at St Giles and a scenic window overlooking Ashdown Forest in the Church Hall. I published 'A History of St Giles Church, Horsted Keynes'. In February 2011 after two gruelling winters Elsie (89) came down from Settle to join us with James in Horsted Keynes Rectory and settled well into village life. Our friend John Harris helped me clear Elsie's flat, its sale marking the end of an era for Twisleton residence in Settle. In 2013 I was made Canon by Fr Cornell Moss, the Bishop of Guyana, marking our contribution to training priests there. James started that year at Sussex University and Anne's mum Doris left Shipley to live with her older daughter Kath with Brian in Hilton, near Middlesbrough and we ended up clearing out her home of 50 years. With Elsie choosing to retire to St Anne's convent home in Burgess Hill and James leaving us for digs in Brighton, where he was studying computer science, we were free to retire and move to Haywards Heath. This we did just before my 40th anniversary as a priest, celebrated in St Giles 3rd July 2017.

9   Active retirement

Barbados

We travel to friends
on the island of Barbados
with sea, sand and palms
sparkling in the sun.

Life slows for a fortnight
suiting thirty degrees heat
with a centring of the day
upon a bath in the sea.

The people smile a lot
greeting us on the street
and many speak first hand
of God as real to them.

Their history is ugly.
Britain held slaves here.
Now the island is free
and proud of that.

With its warmth and light
its beauty, its people
and their inspiration
Barbados is second home.

John Twisleton 18 November 2022

After 13 Marylands, Haywards Heath we see Barbados as our second retirement home due to the hospitality of our friends Bishop Wilfred and Ina Wood even if it is made home just two or three weeks a year. With the loosening of commitment to Guyana after the passing of Bishop Cornell Moss we jumped to the Woods' annual invitation to Barbados. This also helps maintain friendships with Canon Noel and Hazel Burke at St David's and the ordinands and staff of Codrington College. A clue to happy retirement is inventing some form of structure which for us has its apex in the late November booking for Barbados. Priests retiring from being parish priests gain a new lease of life freed from pastoral and administrative responsibilities which have this same apex with the widespread secular anticipation of Christmas and the work it entails for clergy. Since retirement Anne and I have deliberately switched carol services for sea baths! It's great to be a priest - celebrant, preacher, confessor, spiritual director etc - and not a fundraiser, volunteer gatherer, meeting attender, property surveyor and carol service convenor as well!

2016 saw us beginning to itemise and dispose of 75% of the furniture and possessions which had accumulated in The Rectory in Horsted Keynes. John's major practical challenge was disposing of 500 out of 2000 books or booklets to fit our new premises - yes you can shelve a box room to host 1500 books with a desk and window altar! John's mother's move in with us had brought even more "stuff". We categorised everything - keep, dump, sell, give away, and John listed everything electronically, and if an item did not attract interest, he immediately reduced the price until someone bought it. That way, the buyer had to come and take away things like a big freezer, the washer, drier, beds, chairs, tables - some of which had to be carried two storeys down. We felt lighter with every buyer, and it did make us some money. We had a couple of yard sales, and many, many visits to the tip. I invited an auctioneer to come and look at the better items, and he gave us a reasonable price for the odd silver spoons, bits of jewellery, and even the bag of copper coins shoved in drawers. I had worked out how much we could pay for a house, and with help from John's mum, and sadly, my own mother's death in 2015 which left me with half of her estate, and by looking in the then poorer end of Haywards Heath (Bentswood) I found a little close nestling around the Church of the Presentation, where the two and three bedroom houses built 30 years ago were within budget, and one was for sale. The estate agent held an open house, and whispered to me that the house would sell, with no haggling, so I put in the offer. I'd noticed on going around the house that the vendors had Christian statues around, Bibles by the bedside, and, having talked after purchase to the sellers, a delightful Indian family, it seems the bid from Father and Mrs Twisleton had felt right to them and to us in more respects than one. After the sale we all had a time of prayer together. We were fortunate to have good friends who wanted to assist us - one of them an architect, John Whiting, another, Caroline Harris who is a designer of office and house interiors, whose husband John gave us many hours of reduced rate work in painting, fixing up and good advice. From the Church's grant to clergy on retirement we were able to build an extension with downstairs toilet and shower, to make better use of the house's footprint. The builders and plumbers were great guys, and it was a joy to be able to choose a kitchen after the many vicarages with their oatmeal cupboards with teak trim and tired decor! Our new home in a friendly Close ended up being peaceful, light and more spacious than we'd imagined.

2017 first year of retirement, we kept cautious about commitments beyond a fresh family-oriented focus. We visited James during his one year placement in Hong Kong going on to Shanghai, a great holiday! Anne got down to learning Mandarin in preparation for our visit whilst, unconnected with China, John learned Mandolin, activities that require creative scheduling - hot rooming! Otherwise writing (John) and painting (Anne) continued along with attending or celebrating daily Mass (John) and weekly Home Group (Anne). We saw a certain structure emerging in our lives whilst keeping space for family and God-sent openings to serve the common good in Haywards Heath. John recovered his prior-Horsted Keynes involvement at St Richard's Haywards Heath and covered a long vacancy at St Bartholomew's Brighton. He started doing more spiritual direction and engaged with the Bentswood community on local history and digital access for older people. Anne recovered her prior-Horsted Keynes involvement at The Point Network Church in Burgess Hill serving on the children's team. Islington-based Dave and Denise, Tori and Robyn joined us with John Junior, based in Burgess Hill and Brighton-based James on a weekend excursion to Settle in November 2017 to mark the end of the centenary year celebrating dialect poet Tom Twisleton (1845-1917). Elsie, then 95, sent a video greeting from St Anne's Residential Care Home in Burgess Hill to be played at the large Twisleton family lunch in the Royal Oak Hotel. John's poem 'Ode to Tom Twisleton' read at Tom's Memorial Service in Holy Ascension Church, Settle is in Appendix 1.

2018 was an eventful family year marking John's 70th birthday with a grand family celebration in the Presentation Church Hall in November prior to our annual flight to Barbados. James graduated earlier in the year and started work for an IT firm in Brighton celebrating the end of his studies with a trip to the USA. We had as usual delightful visits to David, Denise and the girls in London. John Junior moved jobs and started work in the kitchen at The Bent Arms Inn in Lindfield, happy with the friendly team there who have proved so supportive to him over the years. John continued his annual preaching engagement at his old school, Giggleswick, and was more locally kept in demand as a retired priest who can fill in for vacancies. He continued to write and to broadcast on Premier Radio, give spiritual direction and keep involved in supporting local council events especially linked to local history. Anne's painting and sketching was stimulated by the colour and warmth of Barbados.

2019 saw John's mother, Elsie (97) contributing a thoughtful piece on humility to his Premier Radio series touching on the grace needed to live in a residential home. She did well at St Anne's, Burgess Hill, but it cost her in more sense than one. John Junior had a tumultuous year after coming across a stabbing victim close to where we live. He rendered First Aid and was praised by the Judge in the subsequent murder trial for his actions, and recommended for a High Sheriff's award for bravery. Meanwhile on a lighter note Anne and I were privileged in May to spend the inside of a week each in Venice and Florence. We decided to follow the 3 day tour in each city leaving 2 days for expansion into writing and drawing. The whole experience was expansive due to the feel of the cities and the way paintings and exhibits are framed by galleries twice the size as in the UK serving the greatest concentration of art in the world. We had time to digest our tours, draw and write, be part of age old worship in St Mark's in Venice and Florence's Duomo and walks that brought Florentines like Dante, Galileo, Machiavelli, Michelangelo and Rossini alive to us. In August we spent time with Dave and his family at their chalet on the Isle of Sheppey. In September John Junior received a late diagnosis of Autism. He continues to receive our support, now primarily John's since Anne's Alzheimer's diagnosis, along with his thoughtful landlord Gordon Parr and the team at The Bent Arms in Lindfield where he works in the kitchen.

Anne & John Cockerham with Doris & Ervin Scott c1987

Elsie and John Twisleton en route to Austria 1984

St Wilfrith, Moorends Walsingham pilgrimage c1986

John Twisleton with John & David Cockerham at The College of Ascension, Selly Oak, Birmingham 1987

Marriage of John & Anne Twisleton, St Mary's Church
Yupukari, Rupununi, Guyana 1988

Alan Knight Training Centre ordinands with the Principal Fr John and Vice Principal Fr Allan Buik 1987

Rancher Diane McTurk with giant otters about 1989

John, David, Anne, Fr John & Anthony James Twisleton
outside St Luke's Vicarage, Holbrooks, Coventry c1992

'The Edmonton Walk' 1999 millennium project beating the bounds of Barnet, Camden, Enfield & Haringey and walking to Walsingham organised by Fr John Twisleton

Anne Twisleton, Churchwarden and Spanish Church planter at St James, Muswell Hill about 1998

David Twisleton and Denise Ward about 1998

Caritas 08 Chichester diocesan eucharist organised in
Brighton Centre by Fr John Twisleton with
5,000 attendance, pledging of mission action plans to the
Bishop and sea front procession of witness 2008

Anne Twisleton's 60th birthday in Horsted Keynes 2012

Bluebell Railway Carol Service Horsted Keynes 2013

Tom Twisleton Centenary Service in Settle 2017

Twisleton family reunion at Royal Oak, Settle 2017

James Twisleton and Rebecca Padgham with Henry 2023

Anne and John Twisleton in Barbados 2021

10   Journeying with Alzheimer's

In November 2019 we spoke at a pre-retirement day for clergy, sharing our experience and a few tips about downsizing and living in limited space. We shared how we keep as busy as we want to be, value our prayer and worship times, keep fit in the gym and through walking, see friends and family and look forward to holidays together, and enjoy the friends God sends our way. In the balance of strategy and serendipity we said we were now weighted towards the second, going with the eventful flow and that planning to us was about getting what we want to do in the diary before jumping to other usually welcome demands on our time.

2020 On 13 February John's mother Elsie died, a week after her 98th birthday. A funeral Mass was celebrated by him with family and friends packing the Chapel at St Anne's Convent in Burgess Hill where Elsie passed her last years. The COVID lockdown came two weeks after her funeral so our bereavement was tinged with gratitude. It was not until September that the family reconvened for a weekend in Settle where we were able to lay her remains to rest with those of Greg and Tony in Holy Ascension Churchyard. As a family the trials of that year were softened by good health and continuing employment or furlough for Dave, Denise, John, James and a new family member, Rebecca Padgham now James's fiancée. Like Anne, Rebecca is an artist. During Lockdown we did a lot more walking and in consequence John wrote a bestselling book, 'Fifty Walks from Haywards Heath' which Rebecca illustrated. John was employed through Lockdown as interim Ardingly

College Chaplain ministering to 1100 children sometimes using video. He also kept on providing cover locally online and offered Mass daily in his Oratory with the Bishop's permission on account of the restrictions on public worship put in place. With so many premature deaths John felt led to write a book addressing mortality, 'Pointers to Heaven' with a parallel series broadcast later on Premier Radio. During the COVID lockdown our family was drawn together by a new practice of weekly video conferencing with our children and fortnightly with Anne's sister Kath and husband Brian. Anne saw fresh blossoming of her artwork inspired by the invitation to illustrate Bible stories for online all age teaching offered by The Point Church on YouTube.

2021 It was Anne's return to The Point after Lockdown which first gave public indication of the onset of memory loss though the family were aware through things like misplacement of things at home. Driving to Burgess Hill she got lost trying to find St Paul's College, where this network church is based, a short drive from Haywards Heath. She arrived there one Sunday in the car after a traumatic hour of searching to be consoled by her friends in the children's team. In autumn 2020 a series of falls had put Anne more under the doctor. She encouraged us in spring 2021 to check whether taking antidepressants might solve the memory problems which many were experiencing in the isolating circumstances of Lockdown. This medication did not counter the increasing memory loss. As a family we met up for a long weekend in Yorkshire during August 2021 when a votive candle stand in memory of Elsie was dedicated at Settle Church. Over the weekend James gently challenged Anne over some repetitive conversations to go back to our doctor which she did. In our 2021 pre-Christmas circular Anne wrote days after our return from Barbados: 'The trip was a risk and we took it because lately I have been experiencing some memory loss at times and am in the long queue for a diagnosis'.

2022 Here is our Christmas circular news paragraph written November 2022: 'This has been the year of Anne in two respects, her Alzheimer's diagnosis in May and 70th birthday in September. The former followed two years of indications and nine months of medical investigation concluding with MRI scan and diagnosis. The 70th involved secret preparation by Dave, John and James over four months for the party with some sixty family and friends which was a wonderful surprise to Anne. Dave and Denise's family did us proud with the catering, Tori and Robyn sang and all three boys spoke, as we did, at the celebration. This had a sequence of a weekend in Paris which inspired Anne's lovely painting of the Eiffel Tower as viewed from our hotel. With Anne now unable to drive she switched back to worshipping at All Saints, Lindfield down the road, with lifts from our friend Josie Simpson, interspersed with visits to the Churches John serves and attends: St Richard, Haywards Heath, St Mary, Balcombe, St John the Evangelist, Burgess Hill and St Bartholomew, Brighton. The latter is to be venue for the launch shortly of 'Thirty Walks from Brighton Station', John's main work this year assisted by James and his girlfriend Rebecca. John Junior is starting to serve on the altar at St Richard's and does another excellent service to his dad and mum stepping in as carer one or two days a week helped by rotas devised sympathetically by the chef in the kitchen at Bent Arms. As usual we have just returned from our annual fortnight in Barbados where it is especially easy to live in the here and now, a gift, the seeking of which we find to be the hardest challenge in navigating Alzheimer's disease'.

2023 8 January 2023 was a big day in my life with the launch of 'Thirty Walks from Brighton Station' in St Bartholomew, Brighton after Sunday Mass. It was the fruit of 2 years work and 22 years association with Brighton & Hove and St Bartholomew's. 'Bungaroosh' featured on the cover - James' idea - a composite building material special to Brighton and Hove over the last two centuries. Getting out and about during COVID was a motivator, building on my knowledge of and curiosity about Brighton & Hove built up over the years. So were the enthusiasm of Brightonian James, and his fiancée Rebecca Padgham, who became the book's illustrator building on the work we did together on 'Fifty Walks from Haywards Heath'. In March I went on retreat to Crawley Down monastery praying, among other things, about the struggle we have with Alzheimer's. A remarkable insight came to me linked to the Holy Spirit about how God can work through dementia where there's faith in him. When memory fades you live more in the present moment. This means being left behind somewhat by family and friends with busy diaries and work and recreational commitments. I recalled a book I'd read by the contemporary novelist Santa Montefiore entitled 'Here and Now'. The key figure, Marigold, spent her life taking care of those around her, juggling family life with the running of the local shop, and being an all-round leader in her community. When she finds herself forgetting things the story underlines how she is blessed to dwell more and more with supportive family and friends in the 'here and now' which is the book title. Are we not all meant to attend to every moment of life as best we can, to be as present here and now as we can be? I thought. And *God* - this was my key thought on retreat - *God too is found in the here and now.* Not so much by pondering the past or the future. The Holy Spirit has been defined as 'God in the present moment'. Living with dementia is therefore potentially about living with God and others close to you through rediscovery of the 'here and now' - and the joy of living in God's presence can often be manifested in those suffering this ailment and those who care for them.

The last three years have been a great challenge for both of us. We struggle on, Anne, personable as ever with undimmed joy in the midst of the confusion Alzheimer's disease causes, and myself, somewhat battered and beleaguered. This is through the relentless demands of being responsible for her safety and full time responsibility for our household, cooking, cleaning, laundry and administration, as well as being prime carer for John Junior since his Autism diagnosis. A recent NHS examination said my mood was good for what I'm coping with, possibly linked to my faith. I am not depressed, in need of counselling, but unsettled by countless hour by hour frustrations on account of which I am to be assigned some 'Know Stress' webinars.

John and I are blessed through our faith, our love for one another, our family and the deep friendships we both possess which continue to sweeten our journeying together.

Conclusion

At Anne's 70th birthday in September 2022 our son James paid this tribute to Anne saying: 'Few have lived such a momentous seven decades - few could. Anne Twisleton, who I am fortunate to call my mother, is one of those rarest of individuals imbued with the holy spirit in a way that pours out to everyone she meets... By the grace of God, she met John, my Dad. Anne has been married to John for 34 years... I could talk about Anne's superb creative ability... her talent for lighting a room up and always including people.... What I do want to say is thank you... We're all looking forward to being part of the next chapter in your book!'

We conclude these ten chapters looking forward, as James says, to chapters ahead. Anne and I have journeyed together for half our lives since David and John sought me out as a potential new dad 36 years ago in Birmingham - and we clicked! We were on separate missions but they became *one* mission. The Diocesan Office in Argentina got more sorted, and six Amerindian priests were ordained in Guyana, so we made our mark on South America. We have also made a mark on Doncaster, Settle, Darlington, Shipley, Oxford, Ecuador, Coventry, London and Sussex.

Anne's contributions to countering illiteracy and serving the needs of the poor stand alongside my scientific achievements and Christian writings and the contributions we have both made to young people, church renewal, spiritual direction and spreading the good news of God shown in Jesus Christ.

Alzheimer's disease impacts the capacity to concentrate. This has been more the case with Anne since we started writing this double autobiography in January 2023. I have tried to help by taking what she has already written, or we have written together over the years, and getting her to check, shape or add to the final text. At the core of 'Journeying Together' is a selection we have made of Anne's paintings and that constitutes a third of the book. In the Appendices there are family trees for both of us, articles on the historic Twisleton family and a summary of John's writing, blogging and broadcasts to date.

It seemed good to write together, whilst we could, of so much we have found good and profitable as well as intriguing and challenging in our lives so far. Sustained by Christian faith, we lament what God is allowing to be taken from us through Alzheimer's. In our current situation we put faith in what God provides, here and now, and in the glorious future he has promised and which we would draw others toward in which 'the kingdom of this world with all its anguish is to become the kingdom of our God and of his Christ' (Cf Revelation 11:15b).

Appendix 1 - Family trees

John Fiennes Twisleton - son of Gregory Twisleton and Elsie née Vickers (below)

Twisleton family tree

John Twisleton (b1948) married Anne Cockerham née Scott (b1952) widow of Robert Cockerham (1950-1981), brother of Margaret (b1952). Stepfather of David (b1975 adopted 1992), John (b1977 adopted 1992) and father of James (b1990). Brother of Anthony (1950-1984). Son of Gregory Twisleton (1900-74).

Gregory Twisleton (1900-74) married Elsie Vickers (1922-2020). Brother of Tom Twisleton (1903-1966) married to Marjorie Burton (1909-1995), parents of Greg (1938-1994), married to Gillian Winterbottom (1937-2015), parents of Anne (b1966) married to Mark Jennings, parents of Stefan and Kieran, divorced then married to Phil Boyle, and John (b1969), and Richard (b1944) married to Elaine Smith (b1950), parents of Emma (b1987) and Tom (b1990). Son of Gregory Twisleton (1863-1937)

Gregory Twisleton (1863-1937) married to Jane Holmes (1870-1947). Son of Gregory Twisleton. (1825-1875), married to Jemima Charnley (1836-1883) daughter of Robert Charnley (abt 1790-1864) married to Isabella (abt 1807-1882), grandson of Thomas Twisleton (1777-1841) married to Nanny Batty (1784-1858). Jane Holmes (1870-1947) daughter of Thomas Holmes (b1838) married to Isabella Johnson (b1846) and granddaughter of Thomas Holmes (abt 1810-) married to Betty Richmond (abt 1810-) and John Johnson (abt 1823-) married to Jane Howarth (b1819).

Vickers family tree

John Twisleton (b1948) married Anne Cockerham née Scott (b1952) widow of Robert Cockerham (1950-1981), brother of Margaret (b1952). Stepfather of David (b1975 adopted 1992), John (b1977 adopted 1992) and father of James (b1990). Brother of Anthony (1950-1984). Son of Elsie Twisleton née Vickers (1922-2020).

Elsie Twisleton née Vickers (1922-2020) married Greg Twisleton (1900-1974). Sister of John Vickers (1924-2007) married to Doreen Elliott (1930-2014), parents Paul Vickers (b1958) partner of Gilly Mallett (b1955), parents of Rebecca (b1989), Jack (b1991) and Phoebe (b1996) and of Helen Vickers (b1959) married to Steve Collins (b1961), parents of Grace (b1988), Michael (b1990) and Jenny (b1992). Daughter of Roland Vickers (1890-1934)

Roland Vickers (1890-1934) married Eliza Hagley (1887-1985). Son of John Vickers (b1862) married to Eliza Beddoes (abt 1859-). Grandson of Robert Vickers (abt 1832-) married to Ann Hall (abt 1833-) and Ralph Beddoes (b1821) married to Eliza (b1825). Eliza Hagley (1887-1985) daughter of Robert Hagley (b1854) married to Eliza Gill (b1851) and granddaughter of Thomas Hagley (abt 1801-1892) married to Mary Sanders (abt 1811-) and Edward Gill (abt 1824-) married to Harriet (abt 1825-).

Anne Marjorie Twisleton daughter of Stan/Ervin Scott and Doris Lumley (below)

Scott family tree

Anne Twisleton née Scott (b1952) married John Twisleton (b1948). Widow of Robert Cockerham (1950-1981), brother of Margaret Cockerham (b1952). Mother of David (b1975 adopted 1992), John (b1977 adopted 1992) and James (b1990). Sister of Kathleen (b1948), married to Brian Jones (b1943), mother of Clare (b1972), Emma (b1976) and Sarah (b1983), daughter of Stan/Ervin Scott (1918-2000)

Stan/Ervin Scott (1918-2000) married Doris Lumley (1924-2015). Brother of Norman Scott (b1872) and Eva Scott (b1907) married to Albert Lonsdale (d1972), mother of Ken Lonsdale (b1944), married to Margaret Trimble (b1946), parents of Mark (b1972), Steven (b1974) and Caroline (b1978). Son of Thomas Scott (1875-1940).

Thomas Scott (1875-1940) married Eva Kaye (1882-1957). Brother of Ann Scott (b1872), John Scott (b1873), Robert Scott (b1878) and Sarah Scott (b1880), children of Thomas Scott (d1899) married to Sarah Tinkler. Son of John Scott (b1824) and Mary Young (b1823), grandson of William Scott and Barbara Atkinson (d1870), great grandson of John Scott (b1754) and Ann Todd, great great grandson of John Scott (1694-1775) and Catherine Hubberthorne (d1777). Eva Kaye (1882-1957) daughter of James Kay married to Ellen Evans (1848-1928).

Lumley family tree

Anne Twisleton née Scott (b1952) married John Twisleton (b1948). Widow of Robert Cockerham (1950-1981), brother of Margaret (b1952). Mother of David (b1975 adopted 1992), John (b1977 adopted 1992) and James (b1990), sister of Kathleen (b1948) married to Brian Jones (b1943), mother of Clare (b1972), Emma (b1976) and Sarah (b1983). Daughter of Doris Scott née Lumley (1924-2015).

Doris Scott née Lumley (1924-2015) married Stan/Ervin Scott (1918-2000). Sister of Joyce Lumley (1922-2010) married to Tony/Thomas Raine (d1986), parents of Lydia Raine (b1947), adoptive parent of Aman Lee (b1968), and Andrew Raine (b1955) married to Anna.... , parents of Joel (b1996) and Martha (b1998), brother of Peter Lumley (1930-1935). Daughter of Wilfred Lumley (b1892)

Wilfred Lumley (b1892) married Ethel Barnett (1892-1960). Son of Thomas Lumley (1849-1915) married to Annie Sayer (d1915), grandson of Joseph Lumley (1814-1889) and Martha Fawcett (d1854), great grandson of Thomas Lumley (1759-1836) and Jane Medd (1757-1846), great great grandson of Joseph Lumley (d1781) and Elizabeth Atkinson. Ethel Barnett (1892-1960) daughter of George Barnett (1857-1938) married to Elizabeth Ransome (1856-1943), granddaughter of Bellamy Barnett (1832-1908) married to Sarah Wainwright (1829-1878).

The Twisleton Family

Article by John Twisleton in Settle Community News 2006

When I was at Giggleswick School 1959-66 one of my kinder nicknames was 'Fourth Peak'. This was partly my 6 '3" but partly through the tale of my illustrious forbear and great-great uncle 'The Craven Giant', 22 stone, 7'6" Francis Twisleton (1812-75) whose grave lies in Stainforth Churchyard. 'Fourth Peak' was a good title for a Twisleton since we derive from folk who lived historically in the neighbourhood of the Three Peaks,

Penyghent, Whernside and Ingleborough where you can still find Twisleton Scar, Hall and Glen. There is one other claim to our homeland: Twiston (previously Twisleton) near Blackburn. The name itself means a settlement ('ton') on the fork of a river ('twisla').

In Settle we all know Twisleton's Yard.... There is a reference in the 1871 and 1881 census returns as the residence of our Giant's Aunt Mary and her son, Francis' cousin, Attorney's Clerk James whose grave (1902) is in Settle Churchyard. James' nephew Gregory (1864-1937) ran a store in Settle Marketplace where his son, my own father Greg (1900-74) was born... just up from 'Car & Kitchen'.

At Easter this year, when I enjoyed worship at Holy Ascension with my mother Elsie, I caught the special exhibition at The Folly. This featured among other things two more Twisletons who add colour to our Settle heritage, the craven poets Tom (1845-1917) and Henry Lea (1847-1905).... My father used to read me his favourite from their joint work 'Poems in the Craven Dialect' which was 'Lines composed on Seeing a Woman Intoxicated in Settle Streets on a Market Day'. Our forbears the poets were ardent supporters of the temperance movement. My friends at Settle Social Club know that I am not averse to a pint on my occasional visits. I hope though that any intoxication I get is mainly from the Holy Spirit!

Settle Twisletons trace right back. The West Riding Victoria County History mentions William of Twyselton (1316) holding lands near Ingleborough. Thomas Brayshaw's parish history of Giggleswick refers to Twisletons residing at Sherwood House on the brow beyond Stainforth heading for Horton before 1600. A Robert Twisleton is listed as an enrolled bow man for the battle of Flodden (1513). You can still see the initials RAT 1703 over the porch of Sherwood House referring to Robert and Alice Twisleton who were married 'sexdecimo die Maii 1694' (Giggleswick register). They are pretty certainly my great-great-great-great-great grandparents. My father's poetic great uncles lived up at Winskill (hence the poetry volume 'Splinters struck off Winskill Rock'). It was a pleasure to be reacquainted recently with the current resident of Lower Winskill, an old friend, Tom Lord who inspired me to write this piece to contribute to our local history.

How do the Twisletons of Horton and Settle relate to people like Captain Sir Ranulph Twisleton-Wykeham-Fiennes? There is no easy answer to this. My father and I have kept in touch with Ranulph's uncle, Lord Saye and Sele of Broughton Castle near Banbury and his late brother David Fiennes. Together we are aware that the Twisleton-Wykeham-Fiennes gained their Twisleton through a London goldsmith who worked for Henry VIII, John Twisleton who had a Yorkshire, maybe even a Settle connection. My own middle name is Fiennes which affirms our association with the southern branch of the family....

Family history studies like my own are a resource that can remind us of our history as a community. If we forget it we shall all be the poorer. I end with a quote from 'Stainforth – Stepping stones through history' (2001) which is an excellent production full of great stories. My great-great grandma and great aunt gain a mention: 'In January and February of 1842, there must have been very heavy snowfalls as many villagers lent a hand at a rate of one shilling (5p) a day. Even Nanny Twistleton, a widow 56 years old, living at what is now Fountain House and farming about 34 acres, was probably glad to earn 9d (4p), and he daughter Isabella must have struggled through the snow to get to Langcliffe Mill where she worked as a papermaker'. I myself worked at the same paper mill as a student!

Tom Twisleton Centenary 2017

Foreword to Centenary booklet and commemorative poem by John Twisleton

The warmth and humour of Craven Dialect poet Tom Twisleton (1845-1917) provide a window into the best features and aspirations of Yorkshire.

'Lang Tom fra' Winskill Rock' was literally a giant among men who compensated in humility for his physical aloofness. 'When a chap can't beear from others lips his faults to hear, it shows his want of sense' he writes and his poems poke at self-importance.

Tom Twisleton 100 is a welcome celebration of truth telling in which Settle Stories has partnered the Twisleton family and Settle heritage in working with young people to promote the Craven dialect and engage with social issues.

Tom's poems shine with refreshing integrity. They 'speak truth unto power' shake shackles of addiction and challenge hypocrisy in the name of Truth that sets free.

On behalf of the Twisleton family I am honoured to commend this Centenary publication which points beyond itself to web resources including that 'must read' for Yorkshire folk: 'Poems in the Craven Dialect'.

ODE TO TOM

A century on and your words are still read
for the truth that you tell is undying,
of the beauty of Craven, our dialect, our farming,
the power of speech and of rhyming.

The untruths we live among, some of them new
such as 'post-truth' bring misinformation
so the call for integrity's never been louder.
We need such as you in our nation.

The Truth that sets free was your inspiration.
You spoke and folk saw their deceit.
Many were freed from addiction and wrong
as they willingly sat at your feet.

Your humour and warmth shine out of your poems
as you make yourself one with your fellows
setting forth to them truth which has power in itself
needing whisper or rhyme and no bellow.

'Lang Tom' you lived as a giant among men
but your words are no truth spoken down to us
rather the truth that flows up from the humble
for you are one who lived his life close to us.

Speaking truth unto power you shake off the shackles
of bondage, vain thought and hypocrisy
through allegiance to God whose Truth never errs
and shines out to us through your integrity.

Poem written by Tom's first cousin twice removed Canon Dr John Twisleton of Haywards Heath, West Sussex and read by him at Tom's Memorial Service in Holy Ascension Church, Settle on Sunday 25th September 2017

Appendix 2 - Books, blogs and radio work

Books by the authors

A History of St Giles Church, Horsted Keynes

Besides being the burial place of former UK Prime Minister Harold Macmillan (1894-1986) and mystic ecumenist Archbishop Robert Leighton (1611-1684) St Giles, Horsted Keynes has association with the history of Sussex back to the 8th century. As 53rd Rector (2009-2017) John Twisleton wrote this illustrated history with the assistance of church members.

Baptism - Some Questions Answered

Illustrated booklet on infant baptism used across the Anglican Communion. It explains the commitments involved in baptising a baby, challenges hypocrisy and attempts to clear up a number of misunderstandings in popular culture about what baptism is all about.

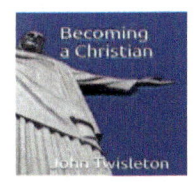

Becoming a Christian

In this booklet John Twisleton clears objections to Christian faith, presents the love of God in Christ and issues a biblical invitation to repent, believe, ask and receive from God. Initiation into the Church is explained and what it means to commit to regular worship, prayer, study, service and self-examination as part of the adventure of faith.

Christianity - Some Questions Answered

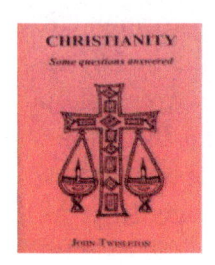

This booklet for Christian enquirers attempts dialogue between Christianity and its contemporary critics. A brief inspection of Christian faith clarifies both its unique claims and its universal wisdom so they can be seen and owned more fully.

Confession - Some Questions Answered

Illustrated booklet explaining the value of sacramental confession as an aid to spiritual growth. It commends confession as a helpful discipline serving people as they struggle against sin and guilt and seek to renew church membership.

Elucidations - Light on Christian controversies

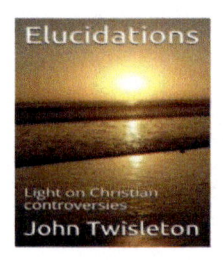

As an Anglocatholic priest who experienced a faith crisis enlarging God for him, John Twisleton, former scientist, sheds light on thoughtful allegiance to Christianity in the 21st century condensing down thinking on controversial topics ranging from self-love to unanswered prayer, Mary to antisemitism, suffering to same sex unions, charismatic experience to the ordination of women, hell to ecology and trusting the Church, a total of twenty five essays.

Empowering Priesthood

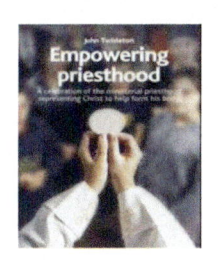

This book is an enthusiastic presentation about the gift and calling of the ministerial priesthood. It argues that the choosing and sending of priests is vital to the momentum of mission and that their representation of Christ as priest, prophet and shepherd is given to help build love, consecrate in truth and bring empowerment to the whole priestly body of Christ.

Entering the Prayer of Jesus

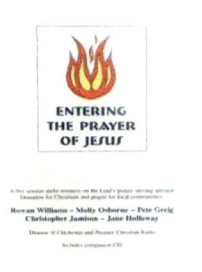

Audio CD and booklet prepared by John Twisleton with the Diocese of Chichester and Premier Christian Radio providing spiritual wisdom from across the whole church. Contains audio contributions from Pete Greig (24-7 Prayer), Jane Holloway (Evangelical Alliance), Christopher Jamison (Worth Abbey), Molly Osborne (Lydia Fellowship) and Rowan Williams (Archbishop of Canterbury).

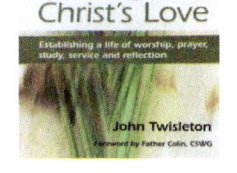

Experiencing Christ's Love

A wake up call to the basic disciplines of worship, prayer, study, service and reflection helpful to loving God, neighbour and self. Against the backdrop of the message of God's love John Twisleton presents a rule of life suited to enter more fully the possibilities of God.

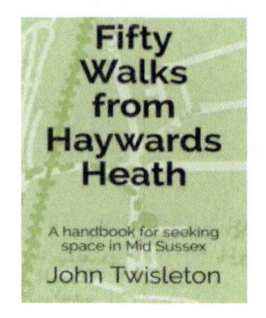

Fifty Walks from Haywards Heath

Sub-titled 'A handbook for seeking space in Mid Sussex' this book celebrates the riches of a town at the heart of Sussex. Through detailed walk routes with schematic illustrations by Rebecca Padgham John Twisleton outlines routes from one to thirteen miles with an eye to local history and replenishment of the spirit.

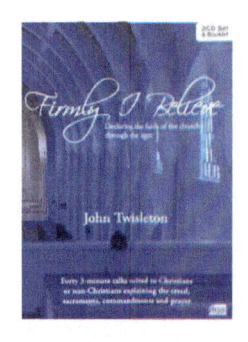

Firmly I Believe

Forty talks suited to Christians or non-Christians explaining the creed, sacraments, commandment and prayer engaging with misunderstandings and objections to faith and its practical expression. Double CD containing 40 easily digested 3 minute talks accompanied by reflective music with full text in the accompanying booklet. Author: John Twisleton.

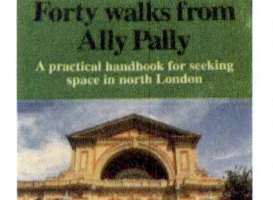

Forty Walks from Ally Pally

John Twisleton explores the byways of Barnet, Camden, Enfield and Haringey with an eye to green spaces, local history and a replenishment of the spirit. The routes, which vary in length between one mile and twenty miles, exploit the public transport network, and are well designed for family outings. The author provides here a practical handbook for seeking space in North London.

Guyana Venture

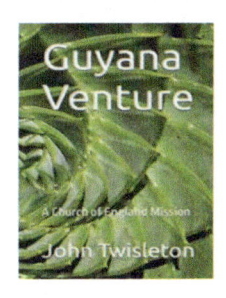

The beauty and challenge of Guyana, formerly British Guiana, has drawn a succession of missionaries from the Church of England to South America. 'Guyana Venture' is framed by John and Anne Twisleton's service there. Mindful of the ambiguities of the colonial past they write proudly of the Church of England venture especially its helping raise up indigenous priests to serve Guyana's vast interior.

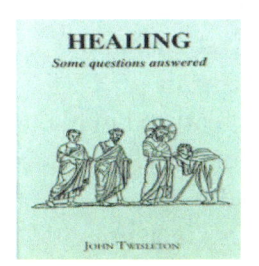

Healing - Some Questions Answered

An examination of the healing ministry with suggested ecumenical forms for healing services. The booklet addresses divine intervention, credulity, lay involvement, evil spirits and the healing significance of the eucharist.

Holbrooks History

Illustrated booklet compiled by John Twisleton with members of St Luke's Church, Holbrooks in Coventry about their parish and its church. It describes a multicultural community that has welcomed Irish, West Indian, Eastern European and Indian workers over the last century. The book includes dramatic pictures from the Second World War when the community and its church suffered bomb damage.

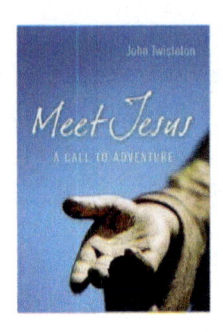

Meet Jesus

In a world of competing philosophies, where does Jesus fit in? How far can we trust the Bible and the Church? What difference does Jesus make to our lives and our communities? Is Jesus really the be all and end all? John Twisleton provides a lively and straightforward exploration of these and other questions pointing to how engaging with Jesus expands both mind and heart.

Mightier than the waves

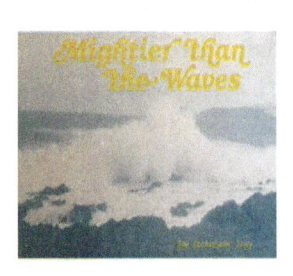

Waves played an important part in the life of Anne Twisleton's first husband, Robert Cockerham, a Christian missionary. Radio waves featured in his work for Radio HCJB (Heralding Christ Jesus' Blessings) in Ecuador and elsewhere. Waves were also instrumental in his death by drowning at the age of 30 in 1981. Anne Twisleton, formerly Cockerham, illustrates and gives the Foreword to this booklet by Geoff Roberts, friend of Robert and Anne, as a tribute to the couple.

Moorends and its Church

Illustrated booklet telling the tale of the Doncaster suburb of Moorends from the sinking of the pit in 1904 to the 1984-5 mining dispute under the theme of death and resurrection. It includes a community survey of the needs of the elderly, young people and recreational and spiritual needs.

Pointers to Heaven

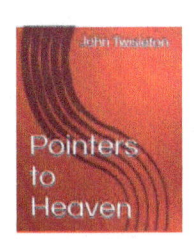

Completed at the height of COVID 19 this book condenses philosophical, theological and life insight into ten pointers to heaven troublesome to materialists: goodness, truth and beauty pointing to perfection alongside love, suffering, holy people and visions pointing beyond this world. If heaven makes sense of earth it is presented as doing so through such pointers, complemented by scripture, the resurrection and the eucharist, preview of the life to come.

Speaking up for Jesus

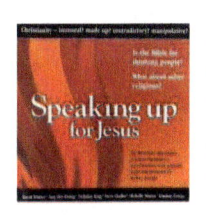

Double CD and booklet with six 20 minute discussions involving Steve Chalke, Cindy Kent, Nicholas King, Michelle Moran, Amy Orr-Ewing, John Twisleton, David Winter and Lindsay Urwin engaging with moral, historical, intellectual and psychological objections to Christian believing, suited to Christians or non-Christians with dramatic input and questions for further thought.

Thirty walks from Brighton Station

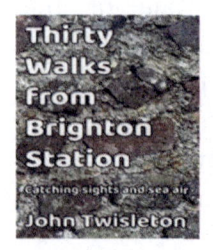

A practical handbook for exploring the city and its surrounds reaching beyond the daytripper's duo of Pier and Pavilion to two hundred and sixty six sights with commentary on many of these. John Twisleton describes his motivation being linked, as a historian, to love for Brighton & Hove, as a walker, to the replenishment of body, mind and spirit attained in that pursuit and as an environmentalist to serving recreation with low carbon footprint. Illustrations: Rebecca Padgham

Using the Jesus Prayer

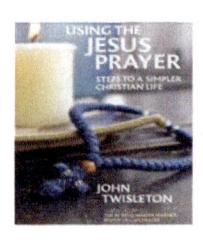

The Jesus Prayer of Eastern Orthodoxy, 'Lord Jesus Christ, Son of God, have mercy on me a sinner' offers a simple yet profound way of deepening spiritual life. John Twisleton gives practical guidance on how to use it outlining the simplification of life it offers.

Blogs

All contemporary blogs can be found on Twisleton.co.uk. Older blogs remain available on blogspot.com and are listed below:

Anglocatholic thinking
https://anglocatholicthinking.blogspot.com/

Anne's gallery https://annespicturegallery.blogspot.com/

Apostles' Creed https://johntwisletoncreed.blogspot.com/

Becket Exhibition https://becketmartyrdom.blogspot.com/

Book of Joy https://tutubookofjoy.blogspot.com/

Book reviews https://johntwisletonreviews.blogspot.com/

Celebrating Haywards Heath
https://lifeinhaywardsheath.blogspot.com/

Downsman's ramblings https://downsman.blogspot.com/

Easter blog https://40resurrectionpointers.blogspot.com/

Elucidations https://elucidatingcontroversy.blogspot.com/

Extraterrestrial life https://lifeawayfromearth.blogspot.com/

Guyana links https://guyanalinks.blogspot.com/

Guyana Venture https://guyanaventure.blogspot.com/

Harold Macmillan https://haroldmacmillan.blogspot.com/

Healthy living https://healthylivingwisdom.blogspot.com/

Making music https://stringedfriends.blogspot.com/

Mystic ramblings https://mysticpondering.blogspot.com/

Night sky https://lookingatnightsky.blogspot.com/

Rail trails https://southdownsrailtrails.blogspot.com/

Richard Rolle - provocative Yorkshire saint
https://strichardrolle.blogspot.com/

Seeing salvation https://seeingsalvation.blogspot.com/

Sights of Barbados https://sightsofbarbados.blogspot.com/

Sights of Bramber, West Sussex
https://sightsofbramber.blogspot.com/

Sights of Brighton & Hove
https://brightonhovesights.blogspot.com/

Sights of Florence https://florencevisit.blogspot.com/

Sights of London https://freelondonfromvictoria.blogspot.com/

Sights of Normandy https://normandysights.blogspot.com/

Sights of Paris https://sightsofparis.blogspot.com/

Sights of Portsmouth https://portsmouthsights.blogspot.com/

Sights of Venice https://venicevisit.blogspot.com/

St Thérèse of Lisieux novena
https://theresenovena.blogspot.com/

Teilhard de Chardin - prophet for today
https://teilhardprophet.blogspot.com/

Thirty Walks from Brighton Station
https://thirtybrightonwalks.blogspot.com/

Thoughts https://johntwisletonthoughts.blogspot.com/

Tom Twisleton https://tomtwisleton.blogspot.com/

Twisleton genealogy https://twisleton.blogspot.com/

Twisleton history https://twisletonhistory.blogspot.com/

Ushaw https://ushaw.blogspot.com/

Vera Lynn https://veraexhibition.blogspot.com/

Why magnify Mary? https://whymagnifymary.blogspot.com/

William Allen and Haywards Heath
https://williamallenhheath.blogspot.com/

Radio work

HCJB Radio based in Ecuador was founded in 1931 to 'herald Christ Jesus' blessings' as the first Christian missionary radio station in the world. It is known also as 'The Voice of the Andes' and was the first station with daily programming in Ecuador. It broadcasts in Spanish and other languages. Listen to the English version at https://uk.radio.net/s/hcjb

Premier Christian Radio based in London launched with analogue-only access in 1994. It expanded to digital accessible worldwide becoming the biggest Christian radio station in the world. It is linked to a telephone counselling service and Christianity monthly magazine. A 2021 UK survey showed 121,000 people tuned in for 3.5 hours a week. Listen to Premier at https://ukradiolive.com/premier-christian-radio

John Twisleton's series on Premier Christian Radio:

Thought of the Day
https://johntwisletonthoughts.blogspot.com/

Entering the prayer of Jesus (5 part series 2005) providing prayer wisdom from Pete Greig (24-7 Prayer), Jane Holloway (Evangelical Alliance), Christopher Jamison (Worth Abbey), Molly Osborne (Lydia Fellowship) and Rowan Williams (Archbishop of Canterbury).

Speaking up for Jesus (6 part series 2006 and CD set) engaging with moral, historical, intellectual and psychological objections to Christianity with Steve Chalke, Nicholas King, Michelle Moran, Amy Orr-Ewing, Lindsay Urwin and David Winter

Firmly I believe (40 part series 2007) on creed, sacraments, commandments and prayer

FAQ on Christianity (40 part series 2008-9)

The Lord is near (4 part Advent series 2013)

Talking points (4 part series 2014) on 'You can't see God', 'All religions lead to God', 'Suffering disproves God' and 'Church is all hypocrisy'

Joy to the world (4 part Advent series 2015)

Seeing Salvation (4 part series November 2016) looking at salvation through scripture, song, teaching and testimony as something personal, practical, purposeful and out of this world.

Jerusalem – City of the Living God (5 part series March 2017) celebrating Jerusalem's role in the record of God's salvation gift in Jesus through scripture and song looking towards the city of the living God, the heavenly Jerusalem.

Experiencing Christ's Love (5 part series November 2017) celebrating Jesus' gracious challenge to love God with heart, soul and mind, and to love neighbour and ourselves, a wake-up call to the basic patterns of worship, prayer, study, service and reflection

Gifts of service (5 part series 2018) celebrating the gifts of hospitality, listening, availability, discernment and humility and the way these gifts are making a difference to individuals and communities.

Bloom in prayer (4 part series 2019) drawing wisdom from Archbishop Anthony Bloom looking at contemplation, the Jesus Prayer, prayer in the Holy Spirit and intercession.

To be a pilgrim (5 part series 2020) getting on the move spiritually through spirited examination of disciplines helpful for treading the path of Christian believing.

Pointers to Heaven (5 part series 2022) inspired by John's book Pointers to Heaven with scripture, song and stories with life experiences pointing to the world to come.

Finding joy in the Lord (5 part Eastertide series 2023) centring on joy as the gift of the risen Lord Jesus to all who put faith in him, seek cleansing from sin and welcome the Holy Spirit into the circumstances of their lives.

More at Twisleton.co.uk

Appendix 3 - Timeline

1948 Birth in Doncaster of John Fiennes Twisleton 29 November

1952 Birth in Darlington of Anne Marjorie Twisleton 17 September

1963 Twisletons move to Giggleswick & Scotts to Shipley

1966 John starts at St John's College, Oxford

1973 Marriage of Anne Scott to Robert Cockerham; John awarded Chemistry Doctorate and called to the priesthood.

1975 Birth in Bradford of David Andrew Cockerham 27 July

1977 Cockerhams move to Ecuador with birth of John Stephen Cockerham 27 December; priestly ordination of Fr John serving as Curate at SS Philip & James, New Bentley, Doncaster within the Company of Mission Priests

1978 Fr John moves to St Wilfrith, Moorends, Doncaster

1981 Death of Robert Cockerham in Ecuador aged 30

1986 Fr John appointed Principal of the Alan Knight Training Centre, Diocese of Guyana, South America. Anne appointed to the Diocesan Office, Buenos Aires, Diocese of Argentina.

1988 John and Anne married in St Mary's, Yupukari, Guyana

1990 Birth in Bradford of Anthony James Twisleton 28 September. Fr John appointed as parish priest at St Luke's Church, Holbrooks, Coventry.

1992 Adoption of John Stephen Twisleton & David Andrew Cockerham Twisleton

1996 Fr John appointed Edmonton Area Missioner, Diocese of London based at 268 Alexandra Park Road in Wood Green. Anne appointed to administrator at Volunteer Reading Help

2001 Fr John appointed Chichester Diocesan Mission & Renewal Adviser based at 27 Gatesmead, Haywards Heath

2002 Anne appointed administrator at All Saints, Lindfield Marriage of David Twisleton and Denise Ward.

2005 Birth of Victoria ('Tori') Twisleton-Ward

2009 Fr John appointed Rector of St Giles, Horsted Keynes near Haywards Heath. Anne appointed as deanery administrator at Chichester Diocesan Family Support Work.

2010 Birth of Robyn Twisleton-Ward

2013 Bishop Cornell Moss appoints John Canon of the Diocese of Guyana

2017 Fr John retires as parish priest with move to 13 Marylands, Haywards Heath. Anne serves on The Point, Burgess Hill children's work team. John assists at St Richard, Haywards Heath with St Bartholomew, Brighton and St John the Evangelist, Burgess Hill

2022 Anne diagnosed with Alzheimer's disease and renews membership at All Saints, Lindfield

2023 James Twisleton engaged to Rebecca Padgham

Printed in Great Britain
by Amazon